Contents

Shells, or Coquilles
Potting
Macaroni
Eggs
Salads
Fritters
Pastry
Canning
Preserves
Pickles and Catchups
Cheese
Sweet Sauces for Puddings
Puddings and Custards
Bavarian Creams
Desserts of Rice
Wine Jellies
Cake
Candies
Ices
Cookery for the Sick

PREFACE.

The aim of this book is to indicate how to serve dishes, and to entertain company at breakfast, lunch, and dinner, as well as to give cooking receipts. Too many receipts are avoided, although quite enough are furnished for any practical cook-book. There are generally only two or three really good modes of cooking a material, and one becomes bewildered and discouraged in trying to select and practice from books which contain often from a thousand to three thousand receipts.

No claim is laid to originality. "Receipts which have not stood the test of time and experience are of but little worth." The author has willingly availed herself of the labors of others, and, having carefully compared existing works—adding here and subtracting there, as experience dictated—and having also pursued courses of study with cooking teachers in America and in Europe, she hopes that she has produced a simple and practical book, which will enable a family to live well and in good style, and, at the same time, with reasonable economy.

The absence from previous publications of reliable information as to the manner of serving meals has been noticed. Fortunately, the fashionable mode is one calculated to give the least anxiety and trouble to a hostess.

Care has been taken to show how it is possible with moderate means to keep a hospitable table, leaving each reader for herself to consider the manifold advantages of making home, so far as good living is concerned, comfortable and happy.

SHELLS, OR COQUILLES.

A TASTEFUL variety at table is a course of something served in shells (*en coquille*). The natural shells (except oyster-shells) are not as pretty as silver shells. Plated silver scallop-shells are not expensive, and are always ready. You can always serve oysters in their shells, by once purchasing fine large ones; then, by cleaning them carefully every time they are used, they will be ready to be filled for the next occasion with suitable oysters from the can. Oysters, lobsters, shrimps, or cold fish of any kind, can be served *en coquille* in place of fish. Chicken, or meat of any kind, should be served as an *entrée*. Salmon, or almost any kind of fish or shell-fish, can be served *en coquille* cold, with a *Mayonnaise* dressing, as a salad.

CHICKENS IN SHELLS.

Boil the chickens in water or in broth; cut the meat into little dice; mix them, while hot, with a hot *Bechamel* sauce, or with a white sauce made with cream; sprinkle sifted bread or cracker crumbs over them; brown slightly in a hot oven. Serve immediately. Sometimes mushrooms are mixed with the chicken dice.

OYSTERS EN COQUILLE.

Prepare oysters as described for *vols-au-vent*; serve them in the scallop-shells, with sifted bread-crumbs (browned) sprinkled over them. Put into the oven until they are thoroughly hot.

FISH EN COQUILLE.

Cut any good fish into little scollops (having boned and skinned them) half an inch wide; fry them in a *sauté* pan, with a little butter, salt, and a few drops of lemon-juice; then mix them with any of the fish sauces, and put them into the shells; sprinkle over bread-crumbs (*sautéd* brown in a little butter), and warm them in the oven.

LOBSTERS OR SHRIMPS EN COQUILLE.

Cut the lobsters into scollops or pieces; mix them with the *Bechamel*, or cream, sauce; sprinkle over bread-crumbs, and brown slightly in the oven.

Proceed in the same manner with shrimps, picking those that are mixed with the sauce, and reserving some whole, to decorate the tops.

Mushrooms en Coquille.

Cut the mushrooms, if they are too large; throw them for a few minutes into boiling water, then into cold water to whiten them; wipe well, and *sauté* them in a saucepan, with a little butter. When colored, and almost done, sprinkle in a little flour and a little chopped parsley; when the flour is cooked (which will require but a few moments), pour in, say, a tea-cupful of stock; let it all simmer for about fifteen minutes. Just before serving, stir in the beaten yolk of an egg, and a few drops of lemon-juice. The sauce should be rather thick. Fill each shell with this mixture; sprinkle a few sifted cracker-crumbs on the tops; brown them slightly with a red-hot shovel, or put them into a very hot oven a few moments just before serving.

POTTING.

In England, potting is an every-day affair for the cook. If there be ham, game, tongue, beef, or fish on the table one day, you are quite sure to see it potted on the next day at lunch or breakfast. It is a very good way of managing left-over food, instead of invariably making it into hashes, stews, etc. These potted meats will keep a long time. They are not good unless thoroughly pounded, reduced to the smoothest possible paste, and free from any unbroken fibre.

Potted Ham.

Mince some cold cooked ham, mixing lean and fat together; pound in a mortar, seasoning at the same time with a little Cayenne pepper, pounded mace, and mustard. Put into a dish, and place in the oven half an hour; afterward pack it in potting-pots or little stone jars, which cover with a layer of clarified butter (lukewarm), and tie bladders or paste paper over them. This is convenient for sandwiches. The butter may be used again for basting meat or for making meat-pies.

Potted Tongue (*Warne*).

Ingredients: One pound and a half of boiled tongue, six ounces of butter, a little cayenne, a small spoonful of pounded mace, nutmeg and cloves each half a tea-spoonful.

The tongue must be unsmoked, boiled, and the skin taken off. Pound it in the mortar as fine as possible, with the spices. When perfectly pounded, and the spices are well blended with the meat, press it into small potting-pans; pour over the butter. A little roast veal, or the breasts of turkeys, chickens, etc., added to the tongue, are an improvement.

Potted Beef.

This is well-cooked beef chopped and pounded with a little butter, pepper, salt, and mace. Manage as for potted ham.

Potted Birds.

Clean pigeons, or any other birds, and thoroughly season them with mace, allspice, pepper, and salt; then lay the breasts in a pan as close as possible, and put some butter over them; cover the pan with a coarse flour paste. Bake the birds well in the oven, and when cold cut them into small pieces; pound these to a paste in a mortar; pack them closely in a potting-pot, and cover with butter.

Potted Fish.

Cut out the pieces of fish; season with pepper, salt, and cloves, if you like; then put them into a dish; cover closely as for potted birds. Bake one hour. When cold, press them into the pot, and cover well with butter, etc.

Potted Chicken and Tongue or Ham.

Roast the chicken; take off all the meat, separating it from the sinews and skin; chop and pound thoroughly, with a pound of tongue or of ham. Let the bones of the chicken be boiled down to a glaze; moisten the pounded meat with this glaze; season with salt, Cayenne pepper, nutmeg, and a little butter. When well pounded and run through a sieve, put it into pots, and press it in hard. Now put the pots into a covered stew-pan, with some boiling water in the bottom; let them be steamed half an hour, then let them cool. Press the meat down again, wipe dry, and cover with some hot butter. It will keep for months.

MACARONI.

MACARONI, WITH CHEESE (*London Cooking-school*).

Do not wash the macaroni. Throw it, broken into convenient pieces, into boiling water which is well salted; stir or shake it frequently, to prevent its adhering to the bottom of the stew-pan. The moment it is quite tender (no longer), pour it into a colander, and shake off all the water. In the mean time, melt a lump of butter the size of a large egg (two ounces) to half a pound of macaroni, in a cup on the fire, and grate a handful (four ounces) of cheese. Now, when the macaroni is well drained, place a little of it in the bottom of the dish in which it is to be served; pour over it some of the melted butter, and sprinkle over that a little grated cheese. Continue alternate layers of the three ingredients until all the macaroni is used, leaving butter and cheese on the top. Put the dish into the oven, and let it remain three or four minutes, or long enough for the macaroni to soak the butter and cheese; then take it out; brown the top with a salamander or hot kitchen-shovel, when it will be ready to be served. Aim to have it done just the moment of serving, otherwise the cheese will cool and harden.[D] It requires about twenty minutes to boil macaroni.

MACARONI AND WELSH RARE-BIT.

When the macaroni is cooked as in the preceding receipt, arrange it in the centre of a large hot platter; brown the top with the salamander; place around it, as a garnish, little diamonds of Welsh rare-bits (see page 264). This is a nice dish to serve in place of cheese.

MACARONI, WITH SWEET-BREADS.

Parboil, egg, bread-crumb, and *sauté* the sweet-breads. Place them in the centre of a large hot platter; arrange macaroni (cooked with cheese) around it, and brown the top with the salamander.

MACARONI, WITH TOMATO-SAUCE.

Sauce.—Put butter size of an egg into a saucepan; when it is at the boiling-point, throw in an onion (minced), two sprigs of parsley (chopped fine), and a little pepper. Let it cook five or eight minutes; then throw in a heaping table-spoonful of flour and a little broth from the stock-pot (if there be no broth, use a little boiling water). Stir this well, and let it cook five or eight minutes longer. Now pour in about a coffee-cupful of tomatoes which have been stewed and strained through a colander or sieve, and stir all together.

Boil half a pound of macaroni tender in well-salted boiling water or in stock, and drain it in the colander. Place alternate layers of the macaroni and the sauce on a hot dish, pouring the sauce over the top; put the dish into the oven two or three minutes to soak the sauce. Serve immediately.

This sauce is simple and very nice. I change it from the receipt of the "London Cooking-teacher," which requires a few additions. His sauce is as follows: Cut a carrot and an onion into little dice, and prepare a bouquet, i. e., tie a little parsley, thyme, and a bay leaf together. Put into a stew-pan some butter (size of a large egg); when it is hot, throw into it the vegetables, bouquet, and three or four whole peppers; let them cook for eight or ten minutes. Then mix in a heaping table-spoonful of flour, and a little of the *pot-au-feu* broth; boil this eight or ten minutes longer; then add a cupful of cooked and strained tomatoes. Stir all together.

MACARONI AU GRATIN (*New York Cooking-school*).

Ingredients: Half a pound of macaroni, four ounces of cheese, two ounces of butter, three-quarters of a cupful of *Bechamel* sauce.

Boil the macaroni as described in "macaroni with cheese." When well drained, pour over it nearly all of the sauce and the grated cheese; toss it in the saucepan, mixing it well together without breaking the macaroni; put it into a *gratin* dish; pour first the remainder of the sauce over the top, then the remainder of the cheese, and over this sprinkle a table-spoonful of cracker-dust and dots of butter. Put it into a very hot oven ten minutes, coloring the top.

CRACKERS, WITH CHEESE.

Soak in boiling water round crackers split in two, three inches in diameter and three-quarters of an inch high (I do not know the name). Take them out carefully, so as not to break them; make layers of these slices in a little *gratin* dish or a deep baking-dish, each slice buttered, spread with a little made mustard, and sprinkled with pepper, salt, and plenty of grated cheese. When all is prepared, bake them in a hot oven for ten minutes.

EGGS.

Boiled Eggs

should all be placed in a wire-basket, and put into boiling water. Boil them two minutes and three-quarters precisely.

Lord Chesterfield said it was only necessary for him to see a person at table to tell if he were a gentleman. He must have had a fine opportunity for observation when boiled eggs were served. It seems nonsense (and it is nonsense) when I say that the fashionable world abroad and their imitators here consider it insufferably *gauche* to serve a boiled egg but in one stereotyped way, *i. e.*, in the smallest of egg-cups. The top of the egg is cut off with a knife, and with a little egg-spoon, dipped into salt when necessary, the egg is eaten from the shell. I really can not see that it matters much whether an egg is eaten from an egg-glass, or in the little egg-cups from the shell, unless one prefers to be in the fashion, when it requires no more trouble.

Poached Eggs.

Salt the water well; when it is *simmering*, drop lightly each broken egg from a saucer into it. Cook one egg at a time, throwing carefully with a spoon the water from the side over the egg, to whiten the top. When cooked just enough (do not let it get too hard), take out the egg with a perforated ladle, trim off the ragged pieces, and slip it on a small, thin piece of hot buttered toast, cut neatly into squares. When all are cooked, and placed on their separate pieces of toast, sprinkle a little pepper and salt over each one.

Some put into the boiling water muffin-rings, in which the eggs are cooked, to give them an even shape; they present a better appearance, however, cooked in the egg-poacher, illustrated among the cooking utensils. Poached eggs are nice introduced into a beef soup—one egg for each person at table; they are also nice served on thin, diamond-shaped slices of broiled ham instead of toast.

Delmonico serves poached eggs on toast, with sorrel sprinkled over the tops.

Poached Eggs on Anchovy Toast.

This is a favorite dish abroad. It is generally a supper-dish, yet can be served at breakfast, lunch, and even as a course for dinner. The dish consists simply of thin pieces of toast, cut of equal size, buttered, and spread with a little anchovy paste, and a poached egg placed on each piece. Anchovy paste can be purchased in little jars at all the larger groceries.

STUFFED EGGS (*for Lunch*).

Boil the eggs hard; cut them in two lengthwise, and remove the yolks, which chop, adding to them some cooked chicken, lamb, veal, or pickled tongue chopped fine; season the mixture, and add enough gravy, or the raw yolk of egg, to bind them; stuff the cavities, smooth them, and press the two halves together; roll them in beaten egg and bread-crumbs twice. When just ready to serve, dip them in a wire-basket into boiling lard; and when they have taken a delicate color, drain. Serve on a napkin, and garnish with parsley or any kind of leaves, or serve with a tomato-sauce.

STUFFED EGGS (*French Cook*).

Boil the eggs hard, and cut them in two; take out carefully the yolks, which mash well, adding a little finely minced onion, chopped parsley, pepper, and salt. Mash also double the quantity of bread, which has been soaked in milk; mix bread, yolks, etc., together; then bind them with a little raw yolk of egg; taste to see if they are properly seasoned. Stuff the eggs with the mixture, so that each half has the appearance of containing a whole round yolk; smooth the remainder of the mixture on the bottom of a pie-pan; arrange the halves symmetrically in this bed; brown a little in the oven.

STUFFED EGGS, WITH CHEESE.

Ingredients: Six eggs, one ounce of cheese, two ounces of butter, one heaping tea-spoonful of flour, a little cayenne, one table-spoonful of vinegar, one and a half cupfuls of milk.

Put the eggs on the fire in cold water, and when they come to a boil set them at the side of the fire to simmer seven minutes; then put them into cold water. When cold, remove the shells; cut them in half lengthwise with a sharp knife, taking care not to tear the whites; mash the yolks, to which add the grated cheese, vinegar, cayenne. At the cooking-school was added also a tea-spoonful of olive oil. Make a *roux* by putting the butter into a little saucepan on the fire, and when it bubbles mix in the flour. In another small saucepan have a wine-glassful of milk boiling, to which add enough of the *roux* to thicken it, and then add the yolks, and mix all together until quite hot. Now to the remaining *roux* add a cupful of milk, and stir until quite smooth for a sauce; fill the cavities of the whites of the eggs with the yolk preparation, rounding the tops to represent whole yolks; arrange them in a circle on a warm platter, and pour the white sauce in the centre.

OMELETS.

Nothing is more simple than to make an omelet, yet very few can make one. The eggs stick to the pan, or they are overdone, and tough.

Senator Riddle, of Delaware, a decided epicure, took much pleasure in his superior knowledge on this important subject. Once when breakfasting with Mrs. Crittenden, of Kentucky, a piece of omelet of doubtful appearance was presented to him. "Before we proceed with our breakfast," said he, "let me teach you a valuable accomplishment." They repaired at once to the kitchen range, where the senator demonstrated at once his qualifications as a first-class cook. My own first lesson was from Mr. Riddle, so of course I have the correct *modus operandi*; afterward in London, however, I heard a lecture upon omelets from a cooking professor, and was astonished at the multiplicity of dishes which could be made from this simple preparation; not only breakfast dishes, but also the variety of sweet omelets for dessert.

Plain Omelet.

The fire should be quite hot. All cookery-books especially expatiate on the necessity of a pan to be used for omelets alone. Any clean, smooth iron spider, or *sauté* pan, is a good enough omelet-pan. Put the pan on the fire to become heated; break the eggs into a kitchen basin; sprinkle over them pepper and salt, and give them twelve vigorous beats with a spoon. This is enough to break all the yolks, and twelve beats was Mr. Riddle's rule. Now put butter the size of an egg (for five eggs) in the heated pan; turn it around so that it will moisten all the bottom of the pan. When it is well melted, and *begins to boil,* pour in the eggs. Holding the handle of the omelet-pan in the left hand, carefully and lightly with a spoon draw up the whitened egg from the bottom, so that all the eggs may be equally cooked, or whitened to a soft, creamy substance. Now, still with the left hand, shake the pan forward and backward, which will disengage the eggs from the bottom; then shaking again the omelet a little one side, turn with a spoon half of one side over the other; and allowing it to remain a moment to harden a little at the bottom, gently shaking it all the time, toss it over on to a warm platter held in the right hand. A little practice makes one quite dexterous in placing the omelet in the centre of the platter, and turning it over as it is tossed from the omelet-pan.

However, if one is unsuccessful in the tossing operation, which is the correct thing, according to the cooking professor, the omelet can be lifted to the platter with a pancake-turner. It should be creamy and light in the centre, and more firm on the outside.

I will specify several different omelets. A variety of others may be made in the same way, by adding boiled tongue cut into dice, sliced truffles, cooked and sliced kidneys with the gravy poured around, etc., etc.

Omelet, with Tomatoes.

Make the plain omelet; and just before turning one half over the other, place in the centre three or four whole tomatoes which have been boiled a few minutes previously and seasoned. When the omelet is turned, of course the tomatoes will be quite enveloped.

Omelet with Green Pease

is managed as omelet with tomatoes, putting several spoonfuls of cooked green pease in the centre before the omelet is lapped, then serving with a neat row of pease (without juice) around it.

Omelet, with Ham.

Throw into the omelet-pan fine-cut shreds of tender ham, with the butter. When the ham has cooked a moment, throw in the eggs, and proceed as for plain omelet. A little chopped parsley beaten with the eggs will improve it. The dish may be garnished with thin diamonds of ham around the omelet.

Omelet, with Fine Herbs.

Before beating the eggs, add with the pepper and salt some chopped parsley and shives; cook a moment in the butter some thin shreds of onion, then pour in the eggs, and proceed as for a plain omelet. The shives may be omitted.

Omelet, with Mushrooms.

Boil the mushrooms in a little water, or stock, to which are added pepper, salt, a few drops of lemon-juice, and, when done, a little flour, to thicken it slightly. Inclose some mushrooms in the omelet in the manner explained for tomatoes; pour the remainder of the mushrooms around the omelet, with a little juice.

Omelet, with Shrimps.

Inclose some picked shrimps in the centre of the omelet. Garnish the omelet with shrimps unpicked.

Omelet, with Oysters.

Scald the oysters in their own liquor; when just about to boil, plump them by throwing them into cold water; then beard them; beat them into the eggs before they are cooked, leaving a few oysters for garnishing the plate.

Omelet, with Cheese, or Fondue.

Brillat Savarin says: "Take the same number of eggs as guests at table. Take then a piece of good *fromage de Gruyère,* weighing about one-third, and a piece of butter one-sixth this weight. Break up and beat your eggs well in a saucepan; then add your cheese and butter grated. Put your saucepan on the fire, and stir with a wooden spoon until the substance is thick and soft; put in a little salt, according to the age of the cheese, and a good sprinkling of pepper, which is one of the positive characteristics of this ancient dish. Serve up on a warm dish. Get some of your best wine from the cellar, which pass around briskly, and you will see wonders."

Gruyère cheese is considered superior to other cheeses in this omelet; yet any kind of American cheese, if highly flavored, is most delicious also, and, I think, quite as good as the Gruyère. I would use fresh cheese, and chop it fine, rather than grate it, and also would not add so much butter. We will say, then, to six eggs add three-quarters of a cupful, or two ounces, of cheese chopped fine, a piece of butter the size of a small egg, salt, and pepper. Proceed as for plain omelet.

Omelet, with Cheese and Macaroni.

Add to the above receipt about two or three cupfuls of macaroni which has been boiled in salted water and drained, and is still hot.

Fried Omelet Soufflé (*for Breakfast*).

Beat the whites and yolks of four eggs separately, and then, adding pepper and salt, put the whites over the yolks, and mix them together carefully. Put butter the size of a small egg into an omelet-pan, and when it has covered the bottom of the pan and is bubbling turn in the eggs; with a spoon lift them from the bottom until all is slightly cooked, or at least well heated; then gather up the sides to make it into omelet form; shake the pan to disengage the omelet, and at the same time to color it slightly at the bottom; turn this over into the centre of a warm platter, so that the colored part be on top.

Sweet Omelet (*for Dessert*).

Add a little sugar to the eggs, instead of pepper and salt; make it then as a plain omelet, inclosing in the centre any kind of preserves, marmalade, or jam; when it is turned on to the dish, sprinkle sugar over the top.

Omelet, with Rum.

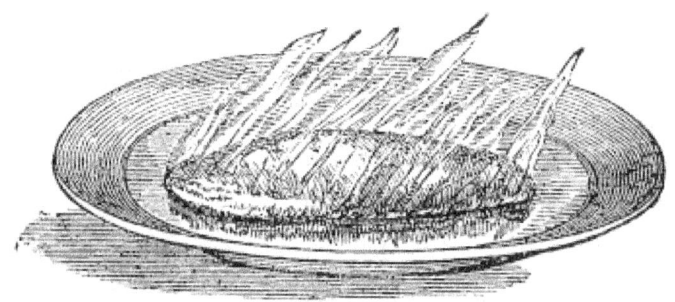

This is a most delicious omelet. Add a little sugar to the eggs, say a sherry-glassful to six eggs, and make the omelet as a plain omelet. When turned on to the dish, sprinkle a little handful of sugar over the top, and pour over five or six table-spoonfuls of rum. Set it on fire, and serve it at the table burning.

Omelet Soufflé.

Although it is a simple thing to make an omelet *soufflé*, and although in France there is not one cook in a score who can not make a delicious one for any and every occasion, I would not advise a careless cook to ever attempt it. The ingredients are: Six whites and three yolks of eggs, three ounces of pulverized sugar (three table-spoonfuls), and a flavoring of vanilla or lemon. First, beat the yolks and sugar to a light cream, and add a few drops of flavoring; then beat the whites to the stiffest possible froth. Have the yolks in a rather deep kitchen bowl; turn the whites over them, and with a spoon, giving it a rotary motion, cut the two, mixing them carefully together. Turn this on to a baking-dish, either of earthenware or tin, with sides two or three inches high and slightly buttered. Smooth over the top, sprinkle over sugar, and put it into a moderate oven. If it has to be turned or moved in the oven, do it as gently as possible. When it has risen well, and is of a fine yellow color, it is ready to be served. It should be served at once, or it will fall.

Omelet *soufflé* was especially nice at the Café Vienna in Paris. This is their cook's receipt: "For one portion," said he, "use the whites of three eggs; beat them well; add one table-spoonful of marmalade cut into fine pieces, or little pieces of fresh peaches; mix with powdered sugar. Bake it on a dish rubbed with butter in a rather quick oven." It seemed as if this was too simple a receipt to be so nice. In another place was a layer of marmalade on the bottom of the dish, with a *soufflé* according to the first receipt, flavored with vanilla, banked over it.

Omelet, with Asparagus Points, Cauliflowers, or other Vegetables.

Cook the vegetables first until they are done, as they will not have time to cook with the eggs. Make them in the same manner described for tomatoes; or the vegetables may be beaten with the eggs. Make a border around the omelet of the vegetables used.

SALADS.

In an English book is told a story of a famous French salad-dresser who began very poor, and made a fortune by dressing salad for dinners in London. He would go from one place to another in his carriage, with a liveried servant, and his mahogany case. This case contained all the necessaries for his business, such as differently perfumed vinegars, oils with or without the taste of fruit, soy, caviar, truffles, anchovies, catchup, gravy, some yolks of eggs, etc. I confess to a lively curiosity as to how these perfumed and scientific mixtures would taste; however, we will be satisfied with the hundred and one ways of arranging our simple and delicious salads, within the comprehension of all.

A Frenchman thinks he can not eat his dinner without his salad. It would be well if every one had the same appreciation of this most wholesome, refreshing, and at the same time most economical dish. It is an accomplishment to know how to dress a salad well, which is especially prized by the fashionable world. The materials used for salads are generally those shown in the list on the following page:

> Lettuce,   Onions,   Cold boiled potatoes,
> Celery,   Garlic,   Cabbage,
> Endive,   Radishes,   Cives,
> Garden-cress,   Beet-root,   Tarragon,
> Sorrel,   Pepper-grass,   Nasturtium blossoms;

or salads of mixed vegetables (*salades en macédoine*), selected from this list of vegetables:

> Cold boiled potatoes,   Olives,   Cucumbers,
> String-beans,   Tomatoes,   Carrots,
> Navy-beans,   Pease,   Truffles,
> Lima beans,   Cauliflower,   Turnips.
> Beet-root,   Asparagus-tops,

Salads are also made of cold boiled fowls or fish, as follows:

> Chickens,   Salmon,   Shrimps,

Lobster,   Prawns,   Sardines.

There are two kinds of dressing which are the best and oftenest used: the *Mayonnaise* and the French dressing. Epicures prefer the simple French dressing for salads served without fish or fowl. For chicken and fish salads, and some vegetables, as tomatoes and cauliflowers, they use the *Mayonnaise* sauce. This arrangement of dressings is almost universal in London and Paris. In America we use the *Mayonnaise* for all salads. I prefer the foreign custom. The simple salad with the French dressing is, after all, the most refreshing and satisfactory, if one has a heavy dinner served before it. The receipts are as follows:

MAYONNAISE SAUCE.

Put the uncooked yolk of an egg into a cold bowl; beat it well with a silver fork; then add two salt-spoonfuls of salt, and one salt-spoonful of mustard powder; work them well a minute before adding the oil; then mix in a little good oil, which must be poured in very slowly (a few drops at a time) at first, alternated occasionally with a few drops of vinegar. In proportion as the oil is used, the sauce should gain consistency. When it begins to have the appearance of jelly, alternate a few drops of lemon-juice with the oil. When the egg has absorbed a gill of oil, finish the sauce by adding a very little pinch of Cayenne pepper and one and a half teaspoonfuls of good vinegar; taste it to see that there are salt, mustard, cayenne, and vinegar enough. If not, add more very carefully. These proportions will suit most tastes; yet some like more mustard and more oil. Be cautious not to use too much cayenne.

By beating the egg a minute before adding the oil, there is little danger of the sauce curdling; yet if, by adding too much oil at first, it should possibly curdle, immediately interrupt the operation. Put the yolks of one or two eggs on another plate; beat them well, and add the curdled *Mayonnaise* by degrees, and finish by adding more oil, lemon-juice, vinegar, salt, and cayenne according to taste. If lemons are not at hand, many use vinegar instead.

Delmonico uses four yolks of eggs for two quart-bottles of oil. It is only necessary, then, to use one yolk for a pint of oil, the egg only being a foundation for the sauce. It is easier, however, to begin with more yolks: many use three of them for a gill of oil. The sauce will not curdle so easily if the few drops of vinegar are used at first, after a very little oil is used. It keeps perfectly well by putting it into a glass preserve or pickle bottle, with a ground-glass stopper. It is well to have enough made to last a week at least. The opportunity of making it may be taken, and adding it to the *Mayonnaise* bottle, when there are extra yolks left, after the whites of the eggs are used for other purposes, such as white cake, corn-starch pudding, etc.

It requires about a quarter of an hour to make this sauce. In summer, the process of making it is greatly facilitated by placing the eggs and oil in the ice-chest half an hour before using them. Sometimes, for the sake of a change, the *Mayonnaise* sauce is made green. It is then called

Sauce à la Ravingote.

Here is Carême's receipt for it: "Take a good handful of chervil, together with some tarragon, and a few cives. When these herbs have been washed, put them into boiling water for five or six minutes, with a little salt; after which, cool, drain, and squeeze them dry. Pound them well, adding a spoonful of *Mayonnaise* sauce; then pass the whole through a sieve, and mix with the *Mayonnaise* sauce. If you find it too pale a green, add a little spinach prepared in the same way."

It is more convenient and simple to add boiled and mashed green pease to the sauce for coloring. The green *Mayonnaise* is sometimes used to spread over a cold boiled fish (marinated). The dish is garnished with lettuce heads. Sometimes, for lobster or fish salads, the *Mayonnaise* sauce is prepared red.

Red Mayonnaise Sauce.

Pound some lobster coral, pass it through a sieve, and mix it with the *Mayonnaise* sauce.

French Dressing.

Ingredients: One table-spoonful of vinegar, three table-spoonfuls of olive-oil, one salt-spoonful of pepper, one salt-spoonful of salt, one even tea-spoonful of onion scraped fine. Many use tarragon vinegar, *i. e.*, vinegar in which tarragon has been soaked.

Pour the oil, mixed with the pepper and salt, over the salad; mix them together; then add the vinegar and mix again. Chaptal says: "It results, from this process, that there can never be too much vinegar: from the specific gravity of the vinegar compared with the oil, what is more than needful will fall to the bottom of the salad-bowl. The salt should not be dissolved in the vinegar, but in the oil, by which means it is more equally distributed through the salad."

This is the usual mode of mixing the salad; but I prefer to mix the pepper and salt, then add the oil and onion, and then the vinegar; and, when well mingled, to pour the mixture over the salad, or place the salad over it, and mix all together. It seems to me to be more evenly distributed in this manner.

Many different combinations can be made to suit the fancy, from the list of salad materials. I will give certain combinations oftenest seen. It must be remembered that salad is never good unless perfectly fresh. It should not be mixed, or brought into the dining-room, until the moment when it is to be eaten.

When preparing lettuce salad, choose the crisp, tender, centre leaves of head lettuce. The kind seen in England and France, called *romaine*, is now much used in New York; it is very crisp and tender. The seeds of this lettuce can be obtained in New York. In the East, tarragon, and endive also, are largely produced, and used to imitate these foreign salads. The tarragon leaves are chopped fine, and mixed in the French dressing (without onion) to use with lettuce. The taste for tarragon is generally an acquired one: I prefer the tarragon vinegar to the fresh leaves, as it has only a slight flavor of the plant.

COMBINATIONS.

1. Lettuce (*French Cook*).

Rub garlic in the dish in which lettuce, with French dressing (without onion), is to be served. Leave no pieces of the garlic—merely rubbing the dish will give flavor enough. The French often use garlic in salads. I would advise, however, the use of the simple French dressing with onion to be mixed with the lettuce leaves, and dispense with the garlic. Use the plain or the tarragon vinegar. Nasturtium blossoms have a most pleasant piquant flavor, and make a beautiful garnish for a salad.

Lettuce, with water-cresses or pepper-grass mixed, and small radishes placed around for a garnish. French or *Mayonnaise* dressing.

3.

Lettuce, with cives mixed, and olives placed around for garnish. French dressing.

4.

Lettuce, with celery mixed (most excellent). Cut the celery into pieces, an inch and a half long; then slice these lengthwise into four or five pieces. Mix with lettuce. French dressing.

5.

Lettuce and sorrel mixed. French dressing.

6.

Lettuce, with anchovies (cut into thin strips as celery) and chopped cives. To vary this dish, prawns and shrimps are used for a garnish; or the anchovies may be left out. French dressing.

7.

Endive alone. French dressing.

8.

Endive, mixed with water-cress. French dressing.

9.

Endive, with celery, beets, and hard-boiled eggs in slices. French dressing. Endive in centre, row of eggs around, then row of beets, then an edge of fringed celery.

10.

Water-cress is good mixed with cold boiled beets. Cut the beets into little dice; garnish with olives. French dressing.

11.

Lettuce and dice of cold boiled potatoes, and cold boiled beets. Potatoes piled in the centre, beets next, and lettuce around the edge of the dish. French dressing.

12. POTATO SALAD.

New small onions sliced, mixed with cold boiled potatoes cut into dice. French dressing. This potato salad is very nice.

Another way is to rub the dish with garlic in which the salad is made. Mix chopped parsley with the potatoes cut into dice. French dressing.

13.

Sliced cucumbers, and sliced new onions. French dressing.

14.

Cabbage alone, with French or *Mayonnaise* dressing.

15. COLD SLAW.

Cut the cabbage not too fine; sprinkle pepper and salt over it, and set it on ice, or in a cool place, to keep it crisp.

Dressing.—Beat the yolks of three eggs, or the whole of two eggs, with five table-spoonfuls of good strong vinegar, two heaping tea-spoonfuls of sugar (three, if the vinegar is very strong), half a tea-spoonful of made mustard, and butter size of an almond. Put these ingredients into a tin cup, and stir them over the fire until they are about to boil, or until they become a smooth paste. Put the mixture one side to become cold, and to remain until just before it is wanted at table; then mix it well with the cold cabbage, and garnish the top with slices of hard-boiled egg.

Cold slaw is especially nice served with fried oysters. Place it in the centre of the warm platter on a folded napkin (a too warm platter would injure it), then make a circle of fried oysters around it. This makes a nice course for dinner.

The salads of vegetables are generally better with the French dressing. They present a better appearance by cutting them with a small vegetable-cutter,

16. SALAD OF VEGETABLES (*Salade de Légumes*).

Mix cold boiled pease, string-beans, pieces of cauliflower, asparagus-tops, or almost any one of the small vegetables; do not cut the larger ones too fine. French dressing.

17.

Cold boiled potatoes, Lima beans, beets, carrots. French dressing.

18.

Cold baked navy beans, with *Mayonnaise* sauce.

19. Mayonnaise of Cauliflower.

Place some cauliflowers into just enough boiling water to cover them; add a little salt and butter to the water. When cooked, let them become cold; then season them with a marinade of a little salt and pepper, three spoonfuls of vinegar, and one spoonful of oil. Let them then remain for an hour. When ready to serve, pile them on the dish to a point; then mask them with a *Mayonnaise* sauce.

Carême finishes this dish by placing around it a border of *croûtons* of aspic jelly. I can not think that aspic jelly is good enough to pay for the trouble of making it, and I am a particular advocate for dishes that *taste* well. Gouffé arranges around the dish a border of carrots, beets, turnips, or any green vegetables which have been marinated.

20. Tomatoes à la Mayonnaise.

This is a truly delicious dish; it would, in fact, be good every day during the tomato season.

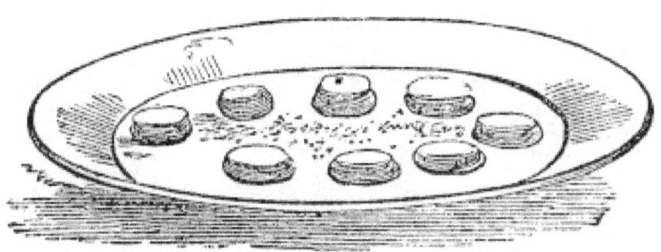

Select large fine tomatoes and place them in the ice-chest; the colder they are, the better, if not frozen; skin them without the use of hot water, and slice them, still retaining the form of the whole tomato. Arrange them in uniform order on a dish, with a spoonful of *Mayonnaise* sauce thick as a jelly on the top of each tomato. Garnish the dish with leaves of any kind. Parsley is very pretty.

Some marinate the tomato slices, *i. e.*, dip them into a mixture of three spoonfuls of vinegar to one spoonful of oil, pepper, and salt; and then, after draining well, mix them in the *Mayonnaise* sauce.

STRING-BEANS IN SALAD (*French Cook*).

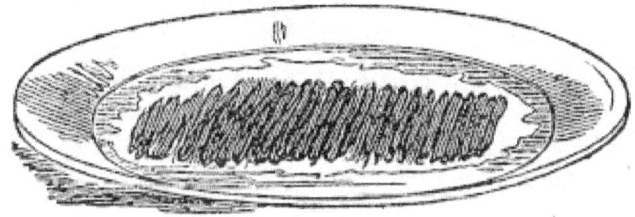

String the beans and boil them whole; when boiled tender, and they have become cold, slice them lengthwise, cutting each bean into four long slices; place them neatly, the slices all lying in one direction, crosswise on a platter. Season them an hour or two before serving, with a marinade of a little pepper, salt, and three spoonfuls of vinegar to one spoonful of oil. Just before serving, drain from them any drops that may have collected, and carefully mix them with a French dressing. This makes a delicious salad.

CHICKEN SALAD.

Boil a young tender chicken, and when cold separate the meat from the bones; cut it into little square blocks or dice; do not mince it. Cut white tender stalks of celery into about three quarter-inch lengths, saving the outside green stalks for soups; mix the chicken and celery together; and then stir well into them a mixture in the proportion of three table-spoonfuls of vinegar to one table-spoonful of oil, with pepper, salt, and a little mustard to taste. Put this aside for an hour or two, or until just before serving; this is called marinating the chicken; it will absorb the vinegar, etc. When about to serve, mix the celery and chicken with a *Mayonnaise* sauce, leaving a portion of the sauce to mask the top. Reserve several fresh ends or leaves of celery with which to garnish the dish. Stick a little bouquet of these tops in the centre of the salad, then a row of them around it. From the centre to each of the four sides sprinkle rows of capers. Sometimes slices or little cut diamonds of hard-boiled eggs are used for garnishing.

Chicken salad is often made with lettuce instead of celery. Marinate the chicken alone; add it to the small tender leaves (uncut) of the lettuce the last moment before serving; then pour *Mayonnaise* dressing over the top. Garnish with little centre-heads of lettuce, capers, cold chopped red beets if you choose, or sliced hard-boiled eggs. Sometimes little strips of anchovy are added for a garnish. When on the table it should all be mixed together. Many may profit by this receipt for chicken salad; for it is astonishing how few understand making so common a dish. It is generally minced, and mixed with hard-boiled eggs, etc., for a dressing.

CHICKEN SALAD (*Carême's Receipt*).

Take some tender pullets; fry them in the sauté pan, or roast them; when cold, cut them up, skinning and trimming them neatly. Put the pieces into a tureen, with some salt, pepper, oil, vinegar, some sprigs of parsley, and an onion cut into slices; mix all well together; cover, and let stand for some hours; then, just before serving, drain the salad, taking care to remove all bits of onion, etc., and place it tastefully on lettuce-leaves, with the hearts of the lettuce on top, and cover with a *Mayonnaise* dressing.

Mayonnaise of Salmon.

Remove the skin and bones from a piece of salmon, boiled and cooled, and cut it into pieces two inches long. Marinate them, *i. e.*, place them in a dish, and season them with salt, pepper, a little oil, and, in this case, plenty of vinegar, some parsley, and a little onion cut up; then cover, and let them stand two or three hours. In the mean time, cut up some hard-boiled eggs into four or eight pieces for a border. Cover the bottom of the salad-dish with lettuce-leaves, seasoned with a French dressing; place your salmon slices in a ring on the lettuce, pouring in the centre a *Mayonnaise* sauce. Sprinkle capers over the whole.

Other kinds of fish, such as pike, blue-fish, and flounders, make very good salads, arranged in the same way. Carême, Gouffé, and Francatelli fry their fish and fowl in a *sauté* pan, instead of boiling them. If you do not make use of remnants of salmon left from the table, you can form better-shaped slices by cutting the fish into little shapes before it is boiled. If you wish to boil them, immerse them in warm water (with vinegar and salt added) in a wire basket, or drainer.

Salad à la Filley.

Ingredients: Cottage cheese, hard-boiled egg, cives.

Arrange cives on a salad-dish in such a manner as to form a nest; put into the nest whole hard-boiled eggs (shelled), one for each person at table, alternated with little round cakes of cottage cheese. In serving, place upon each plate an egg, a cake of cottage cheese, and some of the cives. Each person cuts all together, and puts on the French dressing of oil, vinegar, pepper and salt.

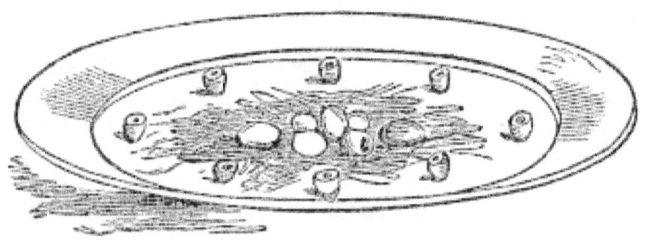

FRITTERS.

French Fritter Batter (*French Cook*), No. 1.

Put a heaping cupful of flour into a bowl; add two yolks of eggs, a table-spoonful of olive oil, which is better than melted butter, and one or two table-spoonfuls of brandy, wine, or lemon-juice.[E] Stir it well, adding, little by little, water enough to give it the thickness of ordinary batter. This may be used at once; but it is better to put it away for a day, or even for a week. At the moment of cooking, stir in well the whites of two eggs beaten to a very stiff froth.

Fritter Batter (No. 2).

Ingredients: One pint of milk, three eggs, a little salt, one pint of flour. It can be made with or without a tea-spoonful of baking-powder.

Beat the eggs well; add part of the milk and salt, then the flour and milk alternately, beating it all quickly, and cooking it immediately, dropping it by the spoonful into boiling-hot lard. The fritters are improved by using prepared flour, Horsford's or Hecker's being especially good.

Pine-apple, Apple Preserve, or Peach Fritters.

Add a pint or less of any of these fruits, cut into small pieces, to either of the above receipts. When done, sprinkle sugar over the tops.

Oyster or Clam Fritters (No. 1).

Chop, not too fine, twenty-five of either clams or oysters (bearded or not), and mix them in the fritter batter of either of the above receipts.

Clam Fritters (No. 2).

Strain one pint of clams, saving the juice; add to this juice sufficient water to make one pint; mix into it one egg, well beaten, and sufficient *prepared* flour to make a light batter, also the clams chopped, and some salt. Drop by the spoonful into boiling-hot lard.

Kentish Fritters (*Mrs. Acton*).

Beat up the whites of three eggs and the yolks of six, with half a pound of flour, a cupful of milk, and a large tea-spoonful of yeast. Put the mixture into a jar, and set it near the stove until the next day; then add to the batter two large apples chopped. Drop this by the spoonful into boiling lard. Sprinkle over sugar.

Fried Cream (*Crême Frite*).

Every one should try this receipt: It will surprise many to know how soft cream could be enveloped in the crust, while it is an exceedingly good dish for a dinner course, or for lunch or tea. When the pudding is hard, it can be rolled in the egg and bread-crumbs. The moment the egg touches the hot lard it hardens and secures the pudding, which softens to a creamy substance very delicious.

Ingredients: One pint of milk, five ounces of sugar (little more than half a cupful), butter the size of a hickory-nut, yolks of three eggs, two table-spoonfuls of corn starch, and one table-spoonful of flour (a generous half cupful altogether), stick of cinnamon one inch long, one half tea-spoonful of vanilla.

Put the cinnamon into the milk, and when it is just about to boil stir in the sugar, and the corn starch and flour, the two latter rubbed smooth with two or three table-spoonfuls of extra cold milk; stir it over the fire for fully two minutes, to cook well the starch and flour; take it from the fire, stir in the beaten yolks of the eggs, and return it a few moments to set them; now, again taking it from the fire, remove the cinnamon, stir in the butter and vanilla, and pour it on a buttered platter until one-third of an inch high. When cold and stiff, cut the pudding into parallelograms, about three inches long and two inches wide; roll these carefully, first in sifted cracker-crumbs, then in eggs (slightly beaten and sweetened), then again in the cracker-crumbs. Dip these into boiling-hot lard (a wire basket should be used if convenient), and when of fine color take them out, and place them in the oven for four or five minutes to better soften the pudding. Sprinkle over pulverized sugar, and serve immediately.

Peach, Apricot, or Apple Frittérs (*French Cook*).

The fresh or the canned fruit may be used. If fresh, pare, core, and cut them in halves. In either case, let them remain two or three hours in brandy, rum, or wine, with plenty of sugar sprinkled over, with some grated lemon peel or zest. When they have absorbed the flavor of these surroundings, drain, and dip them into the fritter batter (No. 1). If rum is used for marinating the fruit, it should be also used in the batter. When the fritters are done and well drained, sprinkle powdered sugar over them.

Bread Fritters.

Having cut off the crust, cut the bread into any shape preferred, such as squares, circles, diamonds, etc. Let it soak in custard (milk, one or two eggs, sugar, and a flavoring of either lemon-zest, or vanilla, cinnamon, nutmeg, rose-water, brandy, or wine). When well soaked (not enough, however, to break into pieces), roll it first in bread crumbs, then in beaten egg (sweetened and flavored), and again in bread or cracker crumbs, and fry in boiling lard. Serve the fritters sprinkled with powdered sugar, with or without a sweet sauce.

Corn Fritters.

Ingredients: The corn cut from seven ears, one pint of milk, one egg beaten, salt, *prepared* flour enough to make a light batter. Drop by the tablespoonful into boiling-hot lard.

Apple Fritters.

Pare some fine apples, and with an apple-corer cut out the core from the centre of each; now cut them across in slices, about one-third of an inch thick, having the round opening in the centre; dip these in either fritter batter No. 1 or No. 2; fry in boiling lard; sprinkle over sugar, and serve in a circle, one overlapping the other, with or without a sweet sauce in the centre.

PASTRY.

Professional cooks use butter for pastry. Puff paste should never be attempted with lard or a half mixture of it. If lard or clarified beef suet is used, the pastry of an indifferent cook will be improved by adding a little baking-powder to the flour and rolling the paste very thin.

It is not difficult to make puff paste. In winter, when it is freezing outdoors, or in summer, when a refrigerator with ice in it is at hand, it is very little more trouble to make puff paste than any other kind. The simple rolling of the dough to form layers requires very little practice. The only secret left, after using cold water and butter cold enough not to penetrate the dough, is to have it almost at a freezing-point, or at least thoroughly chilled, as it is put into a hot oven.

The *vols-au-vent* of strawberries, or berries of any kind, or of jellies, or of lemon paste and also *rissoles*, are especially fine, and are quickly made.

As hundreds of different dishes can be made with pastry, and as Carême has devoted a good-sized volume to the subject, I will copy his receipt for puff paste. It is not modest, perhaps, to put my own first; but it is for the benefit of more ordinary cooks, who will never take extra trouble to make a thing perfect.

Puff Paste.

Ingredients: One pound of flour, three-quarters of a pound of butter, yolks of two eggs, a little salt, a sprinkle of sugar, a little very cold (or, better, ice-cold) water. (All the professional cooks use a pound of butter to a pound of flour. I think it makes the pastry too rich, and prefer three-quarters of a pound of butter to a pound of flour.)

Sift and weigh the flour, and put it on the board or marble slab; sprinkle a little salt and a very little sugar over it. Beat the yolks of the eggs, and then stir into them a few spoonfuls of ice-cold water; pour this slowly into the centre of the flour with the left hand, working it at the same time well into the mass with the tips of the fingers of the right hand. Continue to work it, turning the fingers round and round on the board, until you have a well-worked, smooth, and firm paste. Now roll it out into a rectangular form, being particular to have the edges quite straight. Much of success depends upon the even folding of the paste. Work the butter (which should be kept some minutes in very cold water if it is at all soft) until the moisture and salt are wiped out, and it is quite supple; care must be taken, however, to keep the butter from getting too soft, as in this condition it would ruin the paste. Divide it into three equal parts; spread one part as flatly and evenly as possible over half of the crust, turn the other half over it, folding it a second time from right to left. Roll this out to the same rectangular form as before; spread the second portion of the butter on half of the crust; fold and roll it out again as before, repeating the same process with the third portion of butter. The paste has now been given what they call three turns; it should be given six turns, turning and rolling the paste after the butter is in. However, after the first three turns, or after the butter is all in, the paste should be placed on the ice, or in a cold place, to remain about ten or fifteen minutes between each of the last three turns: this will prevent the butter getting soft enough to penetrate the dough. Each time before the dough is folded, it should be turned half round, so as to roll it in a different direction each time; this makes the layers more even. In order to turn the paste, the end may be held to the rolling-pin; then, rolling the pin, the dough will fold loosely around it; the board may be sprinkled with flour; then the dough can be unrolled in the side direction. This is better than to turn it with the hands, as it should be handled as little as possible. When folded the last time, put the paste on a platter, cover, and place it on the ice for half an hour, or where it may become thoroughly chilled; then roll it out for immediate use; or, so long as it is kept in a half-frozen state, it may be kept for one or two days. Firm, solid butter should be selected for puff paste; a light, crumbling butter would be very unsuitable. After the pies, patties, or other articles are made (as in receipts), the scraps may be used for making rissoles. Always select the coolest place possible for making puff paste. In winter it is well to make it by an open window.

Carême's Receipt for Puff Paste.

Ingredients: Twelve ounces of fine sifted flour, twelve ounces of butter, two drams of fine salt, and the yolks of two eggs beaten.

Manner of working: Having placed twelve ounces of flour on the board, make a small hole in the middle, into which put two drams of fine salt, the yolks of two eggs, and nearly a glass of water. With the ends of the fingers gradually mix the flour with the ingredients, adding a little water when necessary, till the paste is of a proper consistence—rather firm than otherwise. Then lean your hand on the board, and work it for some minutes, when the paste will become soft to the touch and glossy in appearance.

Care must be taken, in mixing the flour with the liquid ingredients, that they do not escape, and that the paste be very lightly gathered together, to prevent it from forming into lumps, which render it stiff, and very difficult to be worked, thereby in some degree causing a failure, which is easily ascertained by the paste, when drawn out, immediately receding, which arises from its having been clumsily and irregularly mixed. To remedy this, let it be carefully rolled out, placing here and there five or six pieces of butter, each the size of a nutmeg, when, after working it as before, it will acquire the degree of softness necessary. It is of importance to observe that this paste should be neither too soft nor too hard, but of a proper medium; yet it is better to be a little too soft than too stiff. One should not choose a hot place in which to make paste: for this reason, summer renders the operation quite difficult. If one can not find a cool place, the paste might be slightly stiffer in summer than in winter.

When the paste has been made as above, take three-quarters of a pound of butter in pieces, which has been twenty minutes in ice-water, well washed and pounded. Squeeze and work it well in a napkin, in order to separate the water from it, and at the same time to render it soft, and, above all, of an equal consistence; then, as quickly as possible, roll the paste into a square on a marble slab (the ends must be perfectly even, as much success depends upon folding); place the butter in the middle; spread it over half the paste, immediately turning over the other half of the paste to cover it. Then roll the paste out about three feet in length; fold it into three parts by doubling one part over the other; after which roll it out again, and fold it once more into three equal parts; now roll it to a greater length, fold it, and put it quickly on a plate sprinkled with flour. Place this upon ten pounds of pounded ice, then, covering it with a second plate, put upon that one pound of broken ice. This plate serves to keep the surface of the paste cool, and also to prevent its becoming soft by the action of the air. After two or three minutes, remove the plate, and turn the paste upside down, instantly covering it as before. After about fifteen minutes, roll it out, and use it as expeditiously as possible.

Thus, in less than half an hour, it is possible to make very fine puff paste, having previously every thing ready—the ice pounded, the butter frozen, and the oven quite hot; for otherwise it can not be done. This is all-important, as it is sometimes an hour before the oven can be made hot. When the oven is half heated, begin to make the paste.

The great variety of elegant and delicate forms[F] this paste is made to assume justifies one for giving such explicit instructions, and repays one for all necessary pains to make it.

For Pies.

I mean Yankee pies. Our English cousins, when speaking of pies, mean only meat-pies, calling our pies tarts. When the paste is fitted over the pie-plate, cut round the edge of it with a sharp knife dipped in flour. Now cut a long curved strip, about three-quarters of an inch wide, wet slightly the top of the paste on the pie-plate near the edge (*not the edge*), and fit the strip around the pie, the edges coming together. Fill the pie, and place in the oven as soon as possible.

Pie Paste of Lard and Butter (*Mrs. Treat*).

Rub a half pound of fresh lard into a pound of flour; use just enough of very cold water to bind it together; roll it out rather thin, and spread butter over the surface; now fold the paste, turning it twice; roll it out again, dredging the board (a marble slab is preferable) with flour; spread on more butter as before, and fold it again. The same process is continued a third time, using in all a quarter of a pound of butter, which should at first be divided into three equal parts.[G]

A Common Paste (*for Meat-pies and Puddings*).

Ingredients: One pound of flour, half a pound of lard, two tea-spoonfuls of yeast-powder, and a little cold water.

First mix well the yeast-powder into the sifted flour; then rub in very carelessly and lightly the lard, distributing it in rather coarse pieces. Now pour in enough cold water to bind it together loosely, using the separated fingers of the right hand to turn the flour lightly, while the water is being poured in with the left hand; roll it out in its rough state; prepare the dish, and bake or boil immediately.

An Apple-pie (*Carême*).

Select fine apples; pare them, and take out the cores without breaking them. Boil several whole in a stew-pan with a little lemon-juice, a very little of the *yellow* part of the peel, some sugar, and enough water to cover them, until nearly done. Quarter other apples; put them also on the fire with a little water, lemon-peel, lemon-juice, and sugar; boil these to a kind of marmalade; add some butter and peach marmalade, and rub it through a colander. Have some pie-plates covered with puff paste; fill the bottom with the marmalade, and put in four small apples (whole) to each pie, filling the cavities between with peach marmalade. Put two strips of crust (half an inch wide) across the pie, which will divide the apples. Bake in a quick oven. This is especially good served with cream.

A Plain Apple-pie (*Miss Amanda Newton*).

Slice pippin apples, and put them between two layers of pie-paste, with enough water to keep them moist. When they are baked, lift the crust carefully off with a knife, and put it aside; now mash the apples with a spoon, season them with plenty of sugar, butter, and grated nutmeg; replace the top crust and sprinkle sugar over it. These pies are especially nice when freshly made, then allowed to cool, and served with cream poured over each piece as it is cut, ready to be eaten.

I think the flavor of the apple is better preserved in this manner than if the seasoning were cooked in it. However, many stew the apples first, before baking them in the pie.

Fruit and Berry Pies, or Tarts.

In England, only an upper crust is made. In this country there is generally only an under crust, with bars of paste crossed over the top. I prefer this mode; but these tarts should always be served fresh, or the under crust will become soaked and unwholesome. The berries or fruits are first stewed with sugar to taste, then baked, or not baked in the crust, as preferred.

Lemon-pie (*Mrs. Hunt*), No. 1.

Ingredients: One heaping table-spoonful of corn starch, one cupful of boiling water, one cupful of sugar, one egg, one table-spoonful of butter, and one small lemon.

Moisten a heaping table-spoonful of corn starch with a little cold water, then add a cupful of boiling water; stir this over the fire for two or three minutes, allowing it to boil, and cook the starch; add a tea-spoonful of butter and a cupful of sugar; remove the mixture from the fire, and when slightly cooled, add an egg, well-beaten, and the juice and grated rind of a fresh lemon. This makes one pie, and should be baked with the crust.

LEMON-PIE (*Long Branch*), No. 2.

Ingredients: Four eggs, four table-spoonfuls of sugar, two-thirds of a cupful of flour, nearly a quart of milk, two small lemons, a little salt.[H]

Bake two under-crusts. Mix the egg-yolks and sugar well together. Bring the milk to the boiling-point, then add the flour mixed with some of the milk, to prevent lumping. Stir it until it has thickened and cooked, when remove it from the fire to stir in the yolks and sugar; return it for a minute to set the eggs; again remove it, and flavor with lemon-juice and grated rind; when the crusts are done, spread over cream, and over this spread the beaten whites of the eggs sweetened and flavored. Put it into the oven a few minutes to color.

ORANGE-PIE (*Mrs. Miller*).

Ingredients: Half a pound of sugar, quarter of a pound of butter, two oranges, six eggs.

Grate the rinds of the oranges, and squeeze the juice. Cream the butter, and by degrees add the sugar. Beat in the yolks of the eggs (already well beaten), then the rind and juice of the oranges. Beat the whites of the eggs to a stiff froth, and mix them lightly in the other ingredients. Bake in paste-lined tin pie-plates.

PUMPKIN-PIE (*Mrs. Otis, of Boston*), No. 1.

Pare a small pumpkin, and take out the seeds; stew it rather dry, and strain it through a colander; add two quarts of milk, three eggs, and three table-spoonfuls of molasses; let the remainder of the sweetening (to taste) be of sugar; season it with two table-spoonfuls of ground cinnamon, one of ginger, and two tea-spoonfuls of salt.

PUMPKIN-PIE (No. 2).

Cut the pumpkin into large pieces, and bake with the skins on; scoop out the soft pumpkin pulp, and proceed as with stewed pumpkin.

MINCE-PIES (*Mrs. Bonner*), No. 1.

Ingredients: Four pounds of lean, cold boiled meat chopped fine, nine pounds of apples chopped fine, one and a half pounds of suet chopped fine, three pounds of raisins, two pounds of currants, half a pound of citron sliced fine, five pounds of sugar, three tea-spoonfuls of ground cloves, ten tea-spoonfuls of ground cinnamon, five tea-spoonfuls of ground mace, one tea-spoonful of ground black pepper, six table-spoonfuls of salt, one quart of cider and vinegar mixed with one quart of molasses.

Mix all, and add the juice and grated rinds of two lemons; or, instead of cider, vinegar, and molasses, one quart of sherry and one pint of brandy may be substituted. Keep this mince-meat in stone jars; add a little more liquor, if it should become too dry, when about to make pies.

MINCE-PIES (*Mrs. Hazard*), No. 2.

Boil, until tender, a beef's tongue which has been kept in salt four or five days; when cold, chop it fine, and add to it two pounds of suet (also chopped fine), two pounds of raisins, two pounds of Zante currants (previously washed and drained), twelve large apples (chopped), four pounds of sugar, the grated rind of one, and the juice and pulp of two large oranges, a cupful of strawberry or of raspberry jam, a cupful of quince preserve, three-quarters of a pound of citron shaved fine, two table-spoonfuls of ground cinnamon, and one table-spoonful of nutmeg. Moisten it with the spiced vinegar from the sweet peach-pickle jar, and add the juice and grated rinds of four lemons.

POTATO-PIE (*Mrs. Osborne*).

Ingredients: Two pounds of boiled potatoes sifted, six eggs, three-quarters of a pound of butter, one pound of sugar, one lemon grated and squeezed into the potatoes while hot, half a nutmeg grated, half a pint of wine, one and a half of rich milk.

Rub the sugar and butter to a cream; add the yolks well beaten, then the potatoes, etc., lastly the whites of the eggs beaten to a stiff froth. Bake with an under crust only.

PINE-APPLE-PIE (*"Choice Receipts"*).

Ingredients: A grated pine-apple and its weight in sugar, half its weight in butter, five eggs (the whites beaten to a stiff froth), one cupful of cream.

Cream the butter, and beat it with the sugar and yolks until very light; add the cream, the pine-apple, and the whites of the eggs. Bake with an under crust. To be eaten cold.

CHESS-PIE.

A gentleman friend spoke to me so often about a wonderfully delicious pie that a lady friend in the country made, that it is not surprising that a person of my culinary tastes should have been very curious. "I will send for the receipt," said I. "But that will not benefit you," he replied, "for I have given the receipt to several of my friends, and they never succeed. Instead of the light production three or four inches high of my country friend, the others are heavy, waxy affairs, very different." I actually took a little journey to see the lady, to get any side explanations from her own lips. I was repaid, as you will see by trying the pie.

Ingredients: For two pies, five eggs, three quarters of a cupful of butter, one cupful of sugar, and necessary flavoring.

Beat the yolks and sugar together until they are a perfect froth. Beat the butter until it is a creamy froth also. Now quickly add them together, flavoring with a little extract of vanilla. Bake it in a crust: it will rise very light. As soon as done, have ready the whites of the eggs beaten to a stiff froth, sweetened with a little sugar, and flavored with a few drops of the extract. Spread this over the tops of the pies, which return to the oven, to receive a delicate coloring.

The lady says the secret of the pies not becoming heavy is in cutting them, and distributing them on the plates, as soon as they are cooked, and still hot; that if they are allowed to cool without cutting them, they will fall. This is rather strange; nevertheless, it seems to be true.

SMALL VOLS-AU-VENT, OR PATTY-CASES.

Make puff paste as before described; give it six or seven turns, wetting the top of the paste, before turning it the last time, with water or a little lemon-juice; roll it out evenly about a third of an inch thick. Cut out as many cakes as are required with a circular tin cutter (a scolloped one is prettier) about two inches in diameter. Now take a second cutter about half an inch smaller in diameter than the first, and press it into the tops of the patties, allowing it to sink half-way through the crust; or cut the patties with a sharp penknife, tracing it around a little paste-board model.

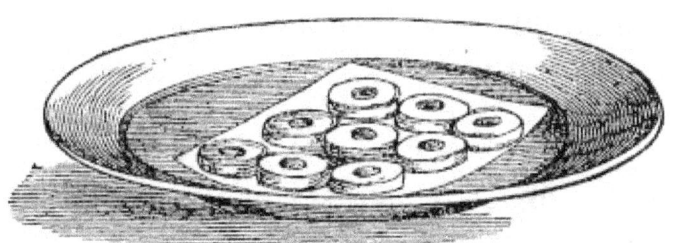

When all are cut, brush over the tops with beaten egg, being careful not to moisten the edges; if they are to be filled with sweetmeats, sprinkle sugar over the tops. When baked, take off the marked-out covers, and cut out the centres without defacing the outsides. Keep them in a warm place until just before serving, when they should be filled, and covered with the little crust tops.

In entertaining, it will be found very convenient to purchase patty-cases at the confectioner's. They can be reheated the last five minutes, and filled with any thing preferred made at home. They are also quite cheap.

OYSTERS FOR VOLS-AU-VENT, SCALLOP-SHELLS, OR SERVED ON BUTTERED TOAST FOR BREAKFAST (No. 1).

Bring a canful or a quart of oysters to the boiling-point in their liquor; then drain them. Put butter the size of half an egg into a saucepan, and when hot add half a small onion (cut very fine) and a tea-spoonful of flour, stirring them well; add then half a tea-cupful of the juice in a can of mushrooms, pepper, salt, a sprig of parsley (cut very fine), half a box of mushrooms (chopped not too fine); then add the oysters. Stir all together over the fire for a minute; add a few drops of lemon-juice. This is a very nice filling for *vols-au-vent* made as in receipt.

OYSTERS FOR VOLS-AU-VENT, SCALLOP-SHELLS, OR SERVED ON BUTTERED TOAST FOR BREAKFAST (No. 2).

Put the oysters on the fire in their own liquor, and when they are just beginning to simmer skim them out quickly with a perforated ladle; if there is too much juice in the saucepan, pour out all except what is necessary for making a sauce of creamy thickness for the oysters; skim this well, and make it as thick as rich cream with flour and butter smoothed together (*roux*). Season it well with salt and Cayenne pepper; some add also a little nutmeg. When cooked enough, take the sauce off the fire, add the yolks of two or three eggs well beaten, and the oysters. Let them merely become hot again on the range without allowing them to boil. Serve immediately. If these preparations are used for scallop-shells, sprinkle some cracker-crumbs over the tops, and brown them quickly with a salamander.

Vols-au-vent of Oysters (No. 3).

Fill the *vols-au-vent* (made as in preceding article) with oysters prepared as follows: Beard and put them into a stew-pan with a little stock; as soon as they are cooked, cut them in two; add three or four table-spoonfuls of the oyster-liquor to the stock, and add to it a *roux* of a little butter and flour; add then a very little cayenne, a little nutmeg, and two or three table-spoonfuls of cream. It should be rather thicker than cream. Fill the pastry the last thing before serving, and cover with the tops.

Vols-au-vent of Sweet-breads.

Prepare the sweet-breads as described in receipt for frying them in the *sauté* pan preparing also the same cream-sauce. After the sweet-breads are cooked, cut them into dice, or into rather small pieces; fill the *vols-au-vent* with them, pouring over them a little of the cream-sauce; cover with the *vols-au-vent* tops.

Vols-au-vent of Chickens, Shrimps, Salmon, Mushrooms, Veal, Game, etc.

Fill the *vols-au-vent* with almost any kind of meat or fish cut into dice, pouring over them a very little sauce. Do not add too much sauce, as it would run through the sides. For chicken, a *Bechamel* or a cream sauce is good; for shrimps, a shrimp-sauce; for salmon or any other kind of fish, Hollandaise, shrimp, pickle, or any fish sauce; for veal or lamb, a little thickened gravy. This is a very good way of using up remnants of any kind of fish or meat.

Vols-au-vent, with Strawberries, Raspberries, or Currants (*English Lady*).

Instead of sprinkling sugar over the tops of the *vols-au-vent,* glaze them on top with four ounces of sugar boiled to a candy, on which sprinkle some fine pieces of pounded loaf-sugar. Take about one-fourth of the ripest of the strawberries to be used, mash them fine, add a little more sugar to what remains of the sugar used for glazing, and after boiling it so that it is not quite ready to candy, add the mashed strawberries and their juice; skim the mixture, and as soon as it sticks to the fingers take it off the fire.

Just before serving, fill the *vols-au-vent* with the fresh strawberries, and cover them with the sirup, when it is cold. Proceed in the same manner with raspberries and red and white currants.

Vols-au-vent, with Strawberries, etc.

When the *vols-au-vent* are nearly or quite done, take them out of the oven, brush the tops over with the white of an egg, then sprinkle over this coarse sugar; return them to the oven to set the glaze. At the moment of serving, fill the *vols-au-vent* with fresh strawberries, raspberries, or any kind of preserved fruit. Place a few spoonfuls of whipped cream over the tops of the fruit.

Lemon Paste (*for Tarts or Patties*).

To one pound of lump-sugar add six eggs, leaving out the whites of two, the juice of four large lemons, with the grated rinds of three of them, and one quarter of a pound of very good butter. Put all into a stew-pan, and stir gently over a slow fire (or set the basin into a pan of boiling water) until it becomes thick and looks like honey; do not let it boil. Pour it into bottles or jars, and keep it in a cool place. It will keep three or four years.

Bake the crust for the tarts. Put in a little of the lemon paste while the crusts are hot. Then return them to the oven, to remain until the paste is nicely melted, when the tarts will be quite ready.

CANNING.

This is a most valuable manner of preserving vegetables and fruits. In cities where vegetables, fruits, or berries are bought at high prices, and perhaps not entirely fresh at that, my experience has taught me that it is cheaper to buy the canned fruits than to have them put up in the house. In the country the expense is very little, as the cans may be purchased in quantities very cheap; and, with proper care in cleaning and drying them, they can be used several times.

The manner of canning one kind of fruit or vegetable applies to almost all kinds, except corn. I would not advise any one to attempt canning corn without the correct process direct from Mr. Winslow himself. By mixing corn and tomatoes together no difficulty will be found. Gumbo and tomato mixed are valuable for soup. Canned tomatoes are invaluable in a household. They are very easily managed, and are as desirable for soups and sauces as for a separate vegetable dish. If fruits or vegetables of any kind are quite fresh, and there is not too large a quantity scalded at one time to prevent careful management of each can, not one can in a hundred will be lost. I also advise the *canning* of sweetmeats of every kind. In that case the same amount of sugar is not required, and the fruit does not have to be boiled until the natural flavor is entirely lost. If glass jars are used instead of cans, they must be put on the fire in cold water with a plate or piece of wood in the bottom of the kettle. They should not be filled until the water is boiling, and then they will not be broken. They should be sealed as soon as possible after they are filled, and when they are cold the covers should again be tightened, as the glass will contract a little after cooling.

To Can Tomatoes.

Let them be entirely fresh. Put scalding water over them to aid in removing the skins. When the cans with their covers are in readiness upon the table, the red sealing-wax (which is generally too brittle, and requires a little lard melted with it) is in a cup at the back of the fire, the tea-kettle is full of boiling water, and the tomatoes are all skinned, we are ready to begin the canning. First put four cans (if there are two persons, three if only one person) on the hearth in front of the fire; fill them with boiling water. Put enough tomatoes in a porcelain preserving kettle to fill these cans; add no water to them. With a good fire let them come to the boiling-point, or let them all be well scalded through. Then, emptying the hot water from the cans, fill them with the hot tomatoes; wipe off the moisture from the tops with a soft cloth, and press the covers on tightly. While pressing each cover down closely with a knife, pour carefully around it the hot sealing-wax from the tin cup, so bent at the edge that the wax may run out in a small stream. Hold the knife still a moment longer, that the wax may set. When these cans are sealed, continue the operation until all the tomatoes are canned. Now put the blade of an old knife in the coals, and when it is red-hot run it over the tops of the sealing-wax to melt any bubbles that may have formed; then, examining each can, notice if there is any hissing noise, which will indicate a want of tightness in the can, which allows the steam to escape. If any holes are found, wipe them, and cover them while the cans are hot with a bit of the sealing-wax. There will be juice left after the tomatoes are canned. Season this and boil it down for catchup.

To Can Peaches.

Cling-stones are best. Pare, halve, and stone them. Boil the stones or pits until all the flavor is extracted; then, having every thing in readiness, as described in the preceding article, pour off the water from the pits, and when it is at boiling-point, throw into it enough peaches to fill three or four cans; sprinkle over sugar to taste, or about as much as would be sprinkled over fresh peaches for the table. When just scalded, can them, placing round pieces of writing-paper dipped in brandy over the tops of the peaches before putting on the covers.

Pears, plums, and all kinds of fruit and berries are thrown into a little boiling water sweetened to taste, scalded, and canned in the same manner as tomatoes.

String-beans.

Next to tomatoes, the vegetable easiest to can is, perhaps, the string-bean. Remove the tough strings at the sides, and break the bean into two or three pieces. When all ready, throw them into a little boiling water, scald, and then can them.

Okra and Tomatoes

are merely mixed and scalded together. Some add pepper and salt, yet these are not necessary in canning. This makes a most delicious soup added to a little stock.

Raspberries

are especially easy to can. They are merely thrown into a little boiling water (which is slightly sweetened), scalded, and then canned. They are very wholesome and nice as a sauce for tea.

Greengages

should be canned without skinning. They should be well scalded in a little sweetened boiling water before canning.

Corn.

Since writing the preceding discouraging remark about corn, I have found, in a Supreme Court decision, Mr. Winslow's receipt for canning corn, as follows:

Fill the cans with the uncooked corn (freshly gathered) cut from the cob, and seal them hermetically; surround them with straw to prevent them striking against each other, and put them into a boiler over the fire, with enough cold water to cover them. Heat the water gradually, and when they have boiled an hour and a half, puncture the tops of the cans to allow the escape of gases, then seal them immediately while they are still hot. Continue to boil them for two hours and a half.

In packing the cut corn in the can, the liberated milk and juices surround the kernels, forming a liquid in which they are cooked.

This process, patented by Mr. Winslow, is by far the best one for preserving the natural flavor of green sweet corn.

Succotash.

Lima beans and corn mixed. They should be boiled until they are thoroughly done.

Corn and Tomatoes

make a good combination for canning. The corn, however, should be thoroughly cooked, and mixed with the tomatoes, after the latter have been scalded merely.

PRESERVES.

To make clear, good preserves requires: 1st. No economy of trouble; 2d. That the fruit be perfectly fresh, *alive* from the tree or bush, or, as a friend says, "tasting of the sun."

The French make the clearest, best preserves, because they spare no pains. They first prepare their sirup or clarified sugar; then, after neatly and carefully paring or dressing their fruit, cook a few pieces at a time, or only as many as they can oversee, carefully lifting each piece out of the sirup the moment it is done. How they preserve strawberries in bottle (each little bottle of which sells for seventy-five cents), retaining the full flavor and almost the firmness of the fresh strawberries, is something for me to investigate.

I consider the peach marmalade the most valuable preserve, as it is useful in preparing desserts. It is a good sauce for almost any kind of pudding, especially corn-starch and rice puddings. Preserves are generally made too sweet. Before hermetically sealed cans or jars were in general use, it required a large quantity of sugar to keep the preserves from fermenting. Now, in using cans, one can suit the taste as to the sweetness of the preserve. I prefer tin cans to glass bottles, as sometimes the bottled jelly or preserves will ferment, requiring a second cooking. Tin cans have never failed me. Others prefer bottles, having no trouble, they say, in tightening them perfectly. The citron preserve, flavored with root ginger and lemon, is a success. It has the flavor of the ginger preserve from the West Indies, which is so fashionable, expensive, and serviceable as an accompaniment for ice-cream, etc.; it is also inexpensive.

Apples preserved with a flavor of lemon and ginger are particularly nice also; of course, they are not as firm as citron, and do not imitate so well the ginger preserve. The outside of the water-melon (skinned) makes a clear, pretty preserve, flavored in the same manner. The next in favor is the greengage preserve, which is as clear and beautiful as it is delicate in flavor. Peaches, unless made into marmalade, are better when canned with very little sugar than when preserved. Canned peaches, half-frozen when served, make a delicious dessert with cake.

First, then, for preserves the sirup must be made. I give the old rule; yet, as before remarked, if canned, they may be made less sweet. I generally use half a pound of sugar to a pound of fruit.

Sirup for Preserves.

Put two pounds of the best white sugar, with one pint of fresh, clear water, into a white porcelain saucepan; put it on the fire, and before the sirup becomes hot mix well into it the partly beaten white of an egg. When it begins to boil, remove the scum as it rises; watch it constantly that it does not boil over; and continue to boil it until no more scum rises.

Now peach, pear, greengage, Siberian crab-apple, and cherry preserves are all made in the same manner. The peaches are neatly peeled, stoned, and halved. The pears are peeled, cored, and cut into two. The greengage makes a prettier preserve without being skinned—pricking them, and halving the stem. The French preserve greengages in this manner. Some think the skins of plums are tough in preserves, and throw them into boiling water to skin them. The Siberian crab-apple, which makes a very good preserve, is cored with a small tin tube or corer (see page 57). Half of the stem is cut from cherries. When the sirup is gently boiling, a few pieces are put into it at one time. They are boiled until they become just soft. Do not allow them to break. When the pieces are done, take them carefully out, and put more into the sirup until all are cooked; pour the sirup over, and put them into jars.

Many add a little juice of lemon to pear, crab-apple, and plum preserves. I would recommend a very little. In the case of peaches, more flavor is gained by boiling the pits, if they are cling-stone (which they should be—the White Heath being the best preserving peach), and after straining the water using it to make the sirup. They will be firmer by laying the uncooked peaches into the sirup, and letting them remain in it overnight, cooking them the next morning. Others harden fruit by letting it remain ten or fifteen minutes in alum-water. This impairs the flavor. However, for good, clear preserves, I prefer the first method of preserving them, using the pits for the water with which to make peach marmalade. Peach marmalade and peach preserves should be made at the same time, when the peaches of less pretentious appearance can be used for the marmalade. Boil preserves without a cover to the kettle.

Citron Preserves (*Miss Leslie*).

The citrons can be pared, cored, and sliced, or cut into fancy shapes with cutters which are made for the purpose. To six pounds of the citron, use six pounds of sugar, four lemons, and a quarter of a pound of ginger-root.

Put the slices of lemon into a preserving-kettle, and boil them for half an hour, or until they look clear, in a little clear water; then drain them. Save the water, and put the slices into another dish with a little cold water; cover them, and let them stand overnight. In the morning wrap the root-ginger (bruised) in a thin muslin cloth; boil it in three pints of clear water until the water is highly flavored, when take out the bag of ginger. Having broken up the loaf-sugar, put it into the preserving-kettle with the ginger-water. When the sugar is all melted, set it over the fire; boil, and skim until no more scum rises. Then put in the pieces of citron and the juice of the lemons. Boil them in the sirup till all the slices are quite transparent. Do not allow them to break. When done, put them into the cans or jars, pouring the sirup carefully over them. If one desires to imitate the West Indies ginger preserve, the slices of lemon may not be added; yet they are a pretty addition.

QUINCE PRESERVES (*Mrs. Hazard*).

Pare, core, and quarter the quinces. Select the best-looking quarters for the preserves; the inferior-looking ones reserve, with the cores and skins, for the marmalade.

For the preserves, allow three-quarters of a pound of sugar to a pound of fruit. Make a sirup as before described (sirup for preserves), allowing one pint of water to two pounds of sugar. When it is clear, and still boiling-hot, add the hot quinces, which have been boiled in just enough clear water to cover them well-boiled until they are tender, or are easily pierced with a broom-straw—no longer. The preserves are now ready to be put away. With this proportion of fruit, water, and sugar, the preserves will not have much juice. What there is will form a thin, clear jelly around the quinces after they are kept a short time: the hot sirup will draw juice from the hot quinces to flavor and color it just enough. There is much difference in the choice of quinces. There is a kind which makes a white or light-colored preserve, very inferior in flavor to the large quince, which makes the red.

TOMATO PRESERVES (*Mrs. Wilson*).

Choose little red, plum-shaped tomatoes, if red preserves are desired, and the small yellow ones for yellow preserves. Peel, and prick them with a large needle; boil them slowly for half an hour in preserving-sirup, with the juice of one lemon to every two pounds of tomatoes; add also a little bag of ginger-root; then skim out the tomatoes; let them remain two or three hours in the sun to harden. Put the white of an egg into the sirup; boil and skim well, and pour it over the tomatoes. The old rule is a pound of sugar to a pound of fruit. I prefer three-quarters of a pound of the former to a pound of the latter. The yellow tomatoes are preferable.

Grape Preserves.

Squeeze with your fingers the pulp from each grape. Put the pulps on the fire, and boil them until they are tender; then press them through a colander, so that the seeds may be taken out; now add the skins to the pulps and juice. Put a cupful of sugar to each cupful of fruit, and boil all together until of a thick consistency. Green-grape preserves are also nice. In managing the green grapes, halve them, and extract the seeds with a small knife. Put also a cupful of sugar to a cupful of fruit. Many prefer the green to the ripe grape preserves.

Apple Ginger.

Boil ginger-root, tied in a thin muslin bag, in clear water until the water is well flavored; make a sirup of this water and sugar, adding to it a little lemon-juice, and allowing three-quarters of a pound of sugar to a pound of apples. When the sirup is skimmed clear, boil in it a few quarters of the apples at a time, until they become clear—no longer. Replace the apples in the sirup when it becomes cold. The golden pippins should be used. This preserve can be made without ginger.

Candied Fruits.

Boil peaches, plums, pears, apricots, cherries, or almost any fruit dressed, in a thick sirup made with a tea-cupful of water to each pound of sugar, until tender—no longer. Let them remain two days in the sirup; then take them out, drain them, and sprinkle sugar over each piece separately. Dry them slowly in the sun or in an oven not too warm.

MARMALADES.

To produce the best marmalades, choose ripe and luscious fruits. Cut them into pieces, and put them into the preserving-kettle with layers of sugar, placing fruit at the bottom.

For marmalades of peach, pear, green grape, pine-apple, quince, or plum, allow three-quarters of a pound of sugar to a pound of fruit. If the fruit is not very juicy, add a little water. Be careful that the marmalade does not burn. When the whole begins to look clear, and becomes thick by cooling a portion of it on a plate, it is done, and may be put into jars at once.

Quince Marmalade.

Save the water in which the quinces for preserving were boiled; add to it the skins and cores, rejecting those which are worm-eaten or discolored. After boiling about half an hour, strain through a colander, allowing the pulp only to pass. To this juice add the reserved quince quarters and the sugar (three-fourths of a pound of sugar to one pound of fruit). Let all boil together slowly for about an hour and a half, stirring occasionally, and breaking the quinces into small pieces. When done, pour it into glasses or bowls. The marmalade will harden, and each mold will form a convenient little dish for lunch.

Peach Marmalade

is made as above. Yet more flavor may be obtained by boiling the pits until their flavor is extracted; then remove them, and continue boiling the water until you have sufficient to add to the peaches.

Orange Marmalade.

Allow three-quarters of a pound of sugar to a pound of fruit. Cut the peels so that they may be removed in four pieces. Boil these peels in a large quantity of water for two hours; then cut them into fine shreds. While these are boiling, press the inside of the oranges through a sieve fine enough to prevent the seeds and skin from passing through. For every five oranges, add the grated rind and juice of one lemon. Put all into a preserving-kettle with the sugar. When done, the marmalade should be quite thick and solid. Cover closely in little preserving-jars.

Raspberry Jam.

Use three-quarters of a pound of sugar to a pound of fruit. First boil the fruit a few minutes with very little water; then add the sugar. Boil three-quarters of an hour, stirring well. Fill little jars or glasses, covering them first with papers soaked in brandy, and then with second papers moistened with the whites of eggs, and pressed against the sides of the glasses to exclude the air.

Greengage Jam.

Use three-quarters of a pound of sugar to a pound of fruit. Skin and stem ripe greengages, and boil them quickly for three-quarters of an hour with the sugar, and only enough water to keep them from burning at first. Skim, and stir very frequently.

Brandy Peaches.

Use cling-stone peaches. Rub off the down from each one, and prick it to the stone with a silver fork. Make a sirup with half a pound of sugar for each pound of peaches, and half a tea-cupful of water for each pound of sugar; also add a little white of egg slightly beaten. Skim, when it boils, as long as the scum rises. Then put in the peaches, boiling them slowly until they are just tender, and no longer; then take them carefully out. Remove the sirup from the fire, and add to it half a pint of the best brandy to a pound of peaches. Now pour this over the peaches. Can them, or put them into jars, well secured.

Apricots and greengages brandied are made in the same way.

To Jelly Fruits.

To make jelly clear, the fruit must be quite fresh, and all blemishes removed. Have the flannels used for straining perfectly clean and white. Nearly all jellies are made in the same way, whether currant, plum, Siberian crab-apple, gooseberry, quince, apple, peach, or grape. Some add less sugar to the sweeter fruits. The first five fruits mentioned are exceedingly easy to jelly; the grape is often quite vexatious, with its perverse inclinations. Cherries will not jelly without gelatine.

After having freed the fruit from all blemishes, put them into a porcelain preserving-kettle, with only enough clear water to keep them from burning at first. Let them boil slowly until quite soft; then, putting them into a flannel cloth, press from them all the juice possible. Strain the juice two or three times through a clean cloth; then return it to the clean preserving-kettle, adding a cup of sugar for every cup of juice, and the beaten white of an egg for the whole. The rule is to boil the sirup (without stirring) very rapidly for twenty minutes, not counting the minutes until it begins to boil. The safest rule is to boil it until it runs a little thick upon the spoon; then let it run through the jelly-bag without pressing it. If there is any fear of the jelly becoming too hard before it all runs through, place it near the fire. The most convenient jelly-strainer is made by fastening the four corners of a flannel cloth to a filter-stool (see page 57). If the first dripping of the jelly is not entirely clear, return it to the strainer until it runs perfectly limpid. Put the jelly into glasses; and, after it has become quite firm, cut out little papers to fit the tops, which should be dipped in brandy. Place over these second papers larger ones, which have been dipped in the whites of eggs. Press the edges against the sides of the glasses, to exclude the air.

CURRANT JELLY.

Follow the preceding directions. A jelly of prettier color is obtained by mixing the white and red currants. Some take the trouble to make jelly from the white and red currants separately, then harden it in successive layers in the glasses. In this way, the jelly has to be made on different days, allowing time for each layer to harden. Another pretty arrangement is to melt the jelly the day before it is served at the table, and put it into a little jelly-mold. The next day it will be quite hard enough to turn out.

CURRANT JELLY (*from Scribner's Monthly*).

"This receipt has three advantages: First, it never fails, as the old plan is sure to do five times out of eight; secondly, it requires but half the usual quantity of sugar, and so retains the grateful acidity and peculiar flavor of the fruit; thirdly, it is by far less troublesome than the usual method. Weigh the currants without taking the trouble to remove the stems; do not wash them, but carefully remove leaves and whatever may adhere to them. To each pound of fruit allow half the weight of granulated or pure loaf sugar. Put a few currants into a porcelain-lined kettle, and press them with a potato-masher, or any thing convenient, in order to secure sufficient liquid to prevent burning; then add the remainder of the fruit, and boil freely for twenty minutes, stirring occasionally to prevent burning. Take out and strain carefully through a three-cornered bag of strong, close texture, putting the liquid into either earthen or wooden vessels—never in tin, as the action of the acid on tin materially affects both color and flavor. When strained, return the liquid to the kettle, without the trouble of measuring, and let it boil thoroughly for a moment or so, and then add the sugar. The moment the sugar is entirely dissolved, the jelly is done, and must be immediately dished, or placed in glasses. It will jelly upon the side of the cup as it is taken up, leaving no doubt as to the result. Gather the fruit early, as soon as fully ripe, since the pulp softens and the juice is less rich if allowed to remain long after ripening. In our climate, the first week in July is usually considered the time to make currant jelly. Never gather currants or other soft or small seed fruit immediately after a rain for preserving purposes, as they are greatly impoverished by the moisture absorbed. In preserving all fruits of this class, if they are boiled until tender or transparent in a small quantity of water, and the sugar is added afterward, the hardness of the seeds, so objectionable in small fruits, will be thus avoided. A delicious jam may be made of blackberries, currants, and raspberries, or with currants with a few raspberries to flavor, by observing the above suggestion, and adding sugar, pound for pound, and boiling about twenty minutes."

Mrs. Walworth's Currant Jelly.

This jelly took the premium at the fair, for it was not only of fine flavor, but of crystal clearness.

An equal proportion of red and white currants was placed in the whitest of porcelain kettles, with a very little clear water, just enough to keep the fruit from burning at first, and was boiled twenty minutes, then poured into a jelly-bag; this was not squeezed or touched until a quantity of clear liquid had run through. (The bag afterward can be well pressed, and the second juice can be made into an inferior jelly.) To each pint of the first clear liquid was added a pound of loaf-sugar; it was then returned to the porcelain kettle (well cleaned), and, after it came to the boiling-point, was boiled twenty-five minutes. The jelly was again passed through the bag, after being well cleaned.

COMPOTES

are fresh fruits boiled when needed, with very little sugar. I consider it a pity to cook or stew peaches, when they are so much better fresh, with sugar sprinkled over them and half-frozen. And what a destruction of fine pears! However, *compotes* are much appreciated and used in France. I value *compotes* of apples, however, and also of inferior hard pears. The first two of the receipts are from Professor Blot.

Sirup for Compotes.

A pound of sugar in a porcelain stew-pan, with a pint of water, a wine-glass of brandy, and a small piece of grated cinnamon. Set it on a slow fire, skimming off the foam; boil it for ten minutes; then, after cooling, bottle it, and by cooking well it will keep for months in a cool, dry place.

Compote of Peaches and Apricots.

Cut the fruit in two; take out the stones; throw them into boiling water (a very little lemon added) for two minutes; then throw them into cold or ice water, taking them out immediately. This makes them white. Then peel them. Put a pint of water into a porcelain pan, and set it on a good fire; when boiling-hot, put in the apricots or peaches, and skim off the foam; as soon as soft, take them out, place them on a dish, and pour over sirup.

Compote of Apples.

Quarter, peel, core, and cook apples in a stew-pan, with a little water and sugar. Take out the apples when cooked. Boil down the sirup (adding sliced lemon and some raisins) to a jelly; then pour it over the apples. Brandy added improves it.

A Beautiful Stuffed Compote.

Choose large fine pippins of equal size; pare them, and take out the cores, leaving the apples entire; cook them about three parts done in sirup; drain and bake them a few moments in a quick oven. When they are done and still hot, fill the interior with peach marmalade. Now roll each apple in jelly produced by boiling down the sirup used to boil the apples; this will give the apples a beautiful gloss. Dish them in pyramidal form; put cream, or whipped cream, or a little maraschino, around the base. Or, form them into a dome, and pour over them a *méringue* of beaten whites of eggs and sugar, sticking regularly over the top sweet almonds cut into four lengths (same size); put it into the oven to brown. This looks like the apple hedgehog. Or, pour among the apples, before pouring over the *méringue*, a marmalade of apples or boiled rice.

PICKLES AND CATCHUPS.

Pickles, for Country Use (*Mrs. Shaw*).

Make a brine strong enough to bear the weight of an egg. Into this put cucumbers fresh from the garden. They will keep in this brine indefinitely. Whenever fresh pickles are wanted, take out as many as are desired from the brine, and let them soak in fresh water two days, changing the water once. Now put two quarts of the best cider vinegar (to fifty cucumbers) on the fire in a porcelain kettle, with one ounce of whole pepper, half an ounce of mustard-seed, one ounce of ginger sliced, half an ounce of mace, a small stalk of horse-radish, a piece of alum the size of a large pea, and half a cup of sugar. Tie up the spices in three muslin bags. Boil all together ten minutes; then pour all over the pickles. It is not necessary to scald the cucumbers, yet many do so, putting them into the kettle, with the vinegar and spices when cold, and covering the bottom, sides, and top closely with cabbage leaves, which improve the color. If they are not green enough at the first scalding, scald them a second time, with fresh leaves around.

This receipt is especially desirable for people living in the country, because, having many vines, the cucumbers of any size preferred can be picked each day, washed, and put into the brine.

Indian Pickle.

Ingredients: To every gallon of vinegar put four ounces of curry powder, four ounces of mustard powder, three ounces of bruised ginger, two drams of Cayenne pepper, two ounces of turmeric, two ounces of garlic, half a pound of onions (skinned), and a quarter of a pound of salt.

Put all into a stone jar. Cover it with a bladder wet with the pickle, and keep it warm by the fire for three days, shaking it well three times a day. Any thing may be put into this preparation, excepting red cabbage and walnuts. Gather every thing fresh, such as small cucumbers, green grapes, green tomatoes, cauliflowers, small onions, nasturtiums, string-beans, etc., etc. Wipe them, cut them when too large, and throw them fresh into the vinegar.

Chowchow Pickle (*Miss Beltzhoover*).

Ingredients: One peck of green tomatoes, half a peck of ripe tomatoes, half a dozen onions, three heads of cabbage, one dozen green peppers, and three red peppers.

Chop them any size you choose, then sprinkle half a pint of salt over them. Put them into a coarse cotton bag. Let them drain twenty-four hours. Put them into a kettle, with three pounds of brown sugar, half a tea-cupful of grated horse-radish, one table-spoonful each of ground black pepper, ground mustard, white mustard, mace, and celery seed. Cover all with vinegar, and boil till clear.

To Pickle Cauliflowers.

Cut the cauliflowers into little flowerets of equal size. Throw them into boiling salted water. Place them at the back of the range, and when they are just about to boil take them off and drain them. Put them into jars. Boil (about fifteen minutes) enough vinegar to well cover them, seasoning it with one ounce of nutmeg, one ounce of mustard-seed, and half an ounce of mace to three quarts of vinegar. Pour this hot over the cauliflowers, adding a little sweet-oil the last thing, to cover the top. Cover them, while warm, with a bladder or fine leather over their corks.

Pickled Walnuts.

Ingredients: One hundred walnuts, salt and water, one gallon of vinegar, two ounces of whole black pepper, half an ounce of cloves, one ounce of allspice, one ounce of root ginger sliced, one ounce of mace.

Gather the walnuts in July, when they are full grown. They should be soft enough to be pierced all through with a needle. Prick them all well through. Let them remain nine days in brine (four pounds of salt to each gallon of water), changing the brine every third day. Drain them, and let them remain in the sun two or three days until they become black. Put them into jars, not quite filling them. Boil the vinegar and spices together ten minutes, and pour the liquid over the walnuts. They will be fit for use in a month, and will keep for years.

Pickled Green Tomatoes and Onions (*Mrs. Monks*).

Chop one peck of green tomatoes, and half a peck of onions. Let them stand two days in layers of salt. Bring vinegar (enough just to cover them) to the boiling-point. Put in the vegetables, mixed with cloves (one ounce), allspice (one ounce), white mustard-seed (two ounces), and red peppers (five large ones shredded). When well scalded, they are ready to be put in jars.

Pickled Onions.

Select small silver-skinned onions. After taking off the outside skins, remove with a knife one more skin, when each onion should look quite clear. Put them into strong brine for three days. Bring vinegar to a boil with one or two blades of mace and some whole red peppers. Pour it hot over the onions well drained from the brine.

Pickled Bell Peppers.

Cut a slit in the side of each pepper, and take out all the seeds. Let them soak in brine (strong enough to float an egg) two days. Then, washing them in cold water, put them into a stone jar. Pour over them vinegar boiled with cinnamon, mace, and nutmeg. Whenever they are wanted to be served, stuff each one with a boiled tongue cut into dice, and mixed with a *Mayonnaise* dressing. Or little mangoes may be made, stuffing each one with pickled nasturtiums, grapes, minced onions, red cabbage or cucumbers, seasoned with mustard-seed, root ginger, and mace.

Ripe Cucumber Pickles.

Pare and seed ripe cucumbers. Slice each cucumber lengthwise into four pieces, or cut it into fancy shapes, as preferred. Let them stand twenty-four hours covered with cold vinegar. Drain them: then put them into fresh vinegar, with two pounds of sugar, and one ounce of cassia-buds to one quart of vinegar. Boil all together twenty minutes. Cover them closely in a jar.

Sweet Pickled Peaches.

To seven pounds of peaches allow three and three-quarter pounds of sugar, one quart of vinegar, two ounces of cloves, and two ounces of stick-cinnamon. Pare the peaches, and stick one or two cloves into each one. Boil the sugar and vinegar, with several sticks of cinnamon, for five minutes, then put in the peaches. When cooked till thoroughly done, take them out. Boil the sirup, reducing it to nearly half, and pour it over the peaches.

Strawberry Pickle.

Ingredients: Seven pounds of strawberries, three and a half pounds of brown sugar, one and a half pints of cider vinegar, one ounce of cloves, one ounce of stick-cinnamon. Place the strawberries and spices in alternate layers in a deep dish. Boil the sugar and vinegar three minutes, and pour it over them, letting them remain until the next day. The second day pour the liquor off and boil it again three minutes, returning it, as before, to the strawberries. Let them remain until the third day, when boil all together over a slow fire for half an hour. Put it away in jars.

Tomato Catchup.

Boil one bushel of tomatoes in a porcelain kettle until soft; press them through a sieve; then add half a gallon of vinegar, two ounces of cloves, one and a half pints of salt, one ounce of Cayenne pepper, five heads of garlic (skinned and chopped), two ounces of whole pepper, one pound of allspice, five ounces of mace, and five ounces of celery seed. Mix all together; and boil until it is reduced to half. Strain, and bottle it.

Tomato Catchup (*Mrs. Cramer, of Troy*).

Ingredients: One peck of tomatoes, two quarts of vinegar, five table-spoonfuls of mustard, five table-spoonfuls of salt, four table-spoonfuls of black pepper, two table-spoonfuls of cloves, three table-spoonfuls of allspice, and two tea-spoonfuls of red pepper.

Let it boil an hour. Strain it through a sieve.

Gooseberry Catchup (*Mrs. Shaw*).

Ingredients: Three pounds of fruit, four pounds of sugar, one pint of vinegar, two ounces of cloves, and two ounces of cinnamon.

Boil all four hours. Bottle it.

Cucumber Catchup.

Grate the cucumbers, and strain off the water through a colander. Add six large onions (chopped very fine) to a gallon of the grated and strained cucumbers. Add vinegar, salt, Cayenne pepper, and horse-radish to taste. Bottle it without cooking.

CHEESE.

In England, and at almost every well-appointed table in America, cheese is a positive necessity to a good table. Brillat Savarin, in his "Physiologie du Gout," says, "Un beau dîner sans vieux fromage est une jolie femme à qui il manque un œil."

Among the best cheeses of England are the Stilton and Cheshire; of France, are those of Neufchatel, Brie (*fromage de Brie*), and the *fromage de Roquefort*. The *fromage de Roquefort* is, perhaps, one of the most popular of all cheeses. The Gruyère cheese of Switzerland is also a well-known cheese. It is made from new milk, and flavored with a powdered herb. In serving this cheese, French mustard, pepper, and salt are usually passed at the same time. The Roquefort cheese is made of a mixture of sheep's and goat's milk: the first communicates consistence and quality; the latter, whiteness and a peculiar flavor. The Parmesan (an Italian cheese) is made of skimmed milk. It is a high-flavored and hard cheese, and is not sent to market until it is six months old, and is often kept for three or four years. It is extensively used, grated, for cooking. The Stilton cheese is made by adding the cream of the preceding evening's milk to the morning's milking, producing a very rich and creamy quality. This cheese is preferred by epicures when it is old, after having been buried for some time in tin cans to become moldy. The Cheshire is made with rich new milk. This cheese can be appreciated without cultivating a taste for it.

Our American cheeses, since the introduction of the factory system, are exported in immense quantities to England, where they are much sought for, and considered by epicures as great luxuries. This is generally astonishing to Americans abroad, who, at home, often consider it only in rule to offer guests cheese of foreign manufacture. I think, however, in comparison with our own, the celebrated foreign cheeses have one advantage. The latter take the name of the exact locality where they are manufactured; consequently, when people speak of a Stilton or of a *fromage de Brie* they know exactly of what they are talking; not so of American cheese. American cheese means that which may be superior, good, bad, or indifferent: it is too general a name. America has hundreds of cheese manufactories, and not a famous one; although many of them make that which would do credit to

America as the greatest cheese-making country in the world, if only these best specimens were more generally known.

I have taken great pains in trying to decide which of many samples is the best American cheese, and have decided upon one made in Otsego County, New York, which is called the "English dairy" cheese. Before proceeding any further, I shall enter my protest against that name. Why do they not call it Otsego cheese? If it were eaten in London, an Englishman would certainly flatter himself that it was made in England. If they will only change the name, then, I will take more pleasure in saying that the Otsego cheese is undoubtedly one of the best specimens of American cheeses. It has a dark-yellow color, is very rich, and highly flavored.

The pastures of Otsego County are exceptionally fine, and its general advantages of climate, etc., render its locality one of the best adapted for the manufacture of cheese.

One of the best specimens of cheese of a milder character, white and well-flavored, is made at Milan, Cayuga County, New York, the name of which might be Cayuga cheese.

Perhaps the cheapest of the foreign famous cheeses is the Neufchatel. It comes in little rolls about an inch thick and three inches long, is enveloped in tin-foil, and costs about twenty cents a roll. Two rolls are quite sufficient for a large dinner. It is a delicious cheese. Care must be taken, however, when purchasing, to ascertain that it is not musty.

The tariff may be saved by purchasing the Neufchatel manufactured in New Jersey and Westchester County, New York. As for that, the Stilton made in Cayuga County can hardly be detected from the Leicestershire manufacture itself; and, in fact, nearly all the famous cheeses are very perfectly imitated in America, so that those who choose may indulge in foreign names and encourage home manufacture at the same time.

In serving Stilton cheese, the top should be cut off to form a cover, and then the cheese should be neatly surrounded with a napkin. Whenever the cheese is taken from the table, the cover should be replaced.

Cheeses are generally cut into little squares and passed in a glass cheese-dish. No morsel of dried cheese should ever be thrown away, as it can be used grated for macaroni, cheese omelets, etc.

Cheese should form a course at dinner. For further particulars concerning cheese as a course, see page 345.

Welsh Rare-bit.

Toast carefully thin square or diamond-shaped slices of bread, with the crust removed. While hot, butter them slightly; then dip them for a moment in a pan containing enough hot water to half cover them; they should be only slightly moistened. Now place each slice on a separate hot plate, allowing one slice for each person at table; sprinkle over a little salt, and pour over them enough melted cheese to cover them. Select rich, new cheese, as it is more easily melted. It can be melted in a little cup. It should not be made until almost ready to serve, as the moment it is finished it should be eaten; otherwise the cheese will harden, the toast will become cold, and the dish altogether will be quite ruined.

This is a favorite dish for gentlemen's suppers or for lunch; yet it is sometimes served at dinner for a cheese course by itself, or for decorating a platter of macaroni with cheese.

This simple receipt is decidedly the best one, I think; yet some spread also a little mustard over the toast, and others add a little ale to the melted cheese. Sometimes the toast may be dipped into ale instead of hot water, and some serve a poached egg on each slice of Welsh rare-bit; still others mix the yolks of eggs into the cheese when melted.

The Welsh rare-bit makes a decidedly pretty course, served in little chafing-dishes in silver, or plated silver, about four inches square, one of which, standing in a plate, is to be served to each person at table. The reservoir contains boiling-hot water; the little platter holds the slice of Welsh rare-bit, which is thus kept hot.

Cottage Cheese.

Place a pan of clabbered sour milk over the fire, and let it become well scalded; then, pouring it into a clean cloth, squeeze out all the water, leaving the clabber quite dry. Put this into a kitchen basin, and work it with the hands, making it a little moist by adding cream. Add also a little butter and plenty of salt; mold it into little balls.

Ramekins (*Ramequins à la Ude, Cook to Louis XVI.*).

Ingredients: Four ounces of grated high-flavored cheese, two ounces of butter, two ounces of bread (without crust), a scant gill of milk, one-third of a tea-spoonful of mustard, one-third of a tea-spoonful of salt, small pinch of Cayenne pepper, yolks of two eggs, whites of three.

Crumb the bread, and boil it soft in the milk; add the butter, mustard, salt, pepper, cheese, and the yolks of the eggs; beat thoroughly; then stir in the whites of the eggs, beaten to a stiff froth. Pour this into little round paper cases (see page 61), which require only a few minutes to make; fill each one about three-quarters full; bake the paste about five or six minutes, when it should be puffed high above the edge of the paper. Serve the ramekins immediately, or they will fall. A good cheese course for dinner, and nice for lunch or supper.

Ramekins, with Ale (*Warne*).

Ingredients: Four ounces of cheese, two ounces of fresh butter, half a French roll, two eggs, half a cupful of cream, half a wine-glassful of good ale.

Boil the roll and cream together until quite smooth; rub the grated cheese and the butter smoothly together; then mix all, adding the ale and the yolks of the eggs well beaten. When the paste is smooth, stir in the whites of the eggs beaten to a stiff froth; put the mixture into paper cases; bake about fifteen minutes, and serve very hot.[1]

Pastry Ramekins (*Warne*).

Ingredients: Some good cheese, puff paste, the yolk of one egg.

Take some puff paste, and roll it out rather thin; strew over it some good grated cheese, and fold it over; repeat this three times, rolling it out each time; then cut the ramekins with a paste-cutter in any form you please, brush them over with the yolk of a well-beaten egg, and bake them in a quick oven for about fifteen minutes. When done, serve them quickly on a hot napkin.

SWEET SAUCES FOR PUDDINGS.

Butter Sauce (*Mrs. Youmans*).

Ingredients: Three-quarters of a cupful of butter, one and a half cupfuls of powdered sugar, four table-spoonfuls of boiling-hot starch, made of flour or corn starch, with either brandy, maraschino, wine, lemon-juice and zest, vanilla, or other flavoring preferred. Stir the butter with a fork to a light cream; add the sugar, and continue to beat it for one or two minutes. Just before serving, stir in with an egg-whisk the boiling starch and the flavoring.

Sirup Sauces.

Boil two cupfuls of sugar with two or three table-spoonfuls of water, until it thickens slightly; take it from the fire; stir in a piece of butter the size of a hickory-nut, and either lemon-juice, fruit-juice, or, in winter, fruit sirups, wine, brandy, or any of the flavoring extracts.

A Plain and Cheap Sauce.

Ingredients: Three and a half cupfuls of water, one cupful of sugar, a small piece of butter, a table-spoonful of either corn starch or flour, flavoring of either brandy, vanilla, lemon, or wine (with or without a little nutmeg), or zest and cinnamon.

When the water boils, stir in the corn starch or flour (rubbed smooth with a little cold water), sugar, and, if used, the yellow rind of a lemon and the cinnamon, and cook well for two or three minutes; take the pan from the fire, and stir in the butter and flavoring (if the lemon and cinnamon are not used).

Same Sauce, Richer (*Mrs. Osborne*).

Ingredients: One pint of water, three table-spoonfuls of flour or corn starch, half a cupful of butter, two cupfuls of sugar, two eggs, half of a nutmeg, half a pint of Madeira or sherry.

Beat the butter and sugar to a cream; add the eggs well beaten, then the nutmeg; heat the wine as hot as possible without boiling; bring the water to a boil in another vessel, and stir in the corn starch or flour (rubbed smooth with a little cold water), and cook it well for about two minutes. Mix well the ingredients off the fire.

Whipped-cream Sauce (*Mrs. Embry, Kentucky*).

Mix a plateful of whipped cream (flavored with wine or vanilla), the beaten whites of two or three eggs, and pulverized sugar to taste, all together. Pile a bank of this mixture in the centre of a platter, and form a circle of little fruit puddings or Swedish puddings (steamed in cups or little molds), *blanc-manges*, corn-starch puddings, etc., around it; or place a large pudding in the centre, with a circle of the sauce around.

Fruit Sauces.

The French bottled apricots, greengage plums, or strawberries make delicious sauces for a Bavarian cream, *blanc-mange, charlotte-russe*, or corn-starch pudding. They may simply be poured around the pudding on a platter, or the juice may, be thickened by boiling it with a very little corn-starch, then adding the fruit to it when cold.

The American canned May-duke cherries (Shrivers) make a good pudding sauce. Boil the juice, and add the slight corn-starch thickening and a little sugar; when cold, add the cherries. It makes a good sauce poured around these puddings.

Fresh red cherries, stewed, sweetened, passed through a sieve, and slightly thickened with corn starch, make another pudding sauce. The Colorado wild raspberries make a fine berry pudding, with the same kind of berry sauce around it. Marmalades and preserves, if not too stiff, make pretty garnishes as well as good sauces.

Strawberry Sauce (*for Baked Puddings*).

Ingredients: Half a cupful of butter, one cupful of sugar, the beaten white of an egg, and one cupful of strawberries (mashed).

Rub butter and sugar to a cream; add the beaten white of the egg, and the strawberries thoroughly mashed.

Boiled Custard

makes a good sauce. If served with plum-pudding, flavor it with brandy; if served with rice-pudding (in mold) or corn starch or other puddings, flavor it with lemon, vanilla, chocolate, or coffee, etc., etc.

A Good Sauce for Puddings (*Miss Amelia Foote*).

Ingredients: Half a cupful of butter, one cupful of sugar, white of one egg, two table-spoonfuls of wine, a little vanilla, and half a wine-glassful of boiling water.

Beat the butter and sugar for about fifteen minutes; then add the flavoring. Just before sending to the table, add the egg, beaten to a froth, and stir in the boiling water, beating it to a foam; or it may be flavored with brandy or wine, without the vanilla.

Sabyllon.

This is a French pudding sauce, and an exceedingly good one. It is so rich that one or two table-spoonfuls poured over a fruit, batter, bread, or almost any kind of pudding, are sufficient. The amount of sauce in the receipt is, therefore, enough for six or seven persons.

Put two yolks and one whole egg, also a scant half tea-cupful of sugar, into a little stew-pan; beat them well for a few minutes. Then put the saucepan into another, containing boiling water, over the fire; beat the eggs briskly with the egg-whisk while you gradually pour in a scant half tea-cupful of sherry; when the sherry is all in, the egg will begin to thicken; then take it from the fire, and add the juice of a quarter of a small lemon.

Caramel Sauce (*New York Cooking-school*).

Dissolve six ounces of cut loaf-sugar in half a pint of boiling water; add a stick of cinnamon, a little lemon-zest, and two cloves, and boil it ten minutes. Next put two ounces of loaf-sugar, dissolved in a table-spoonful of boiling water, on a moderate fire, and stir it until it assumes a light-brown color; pour the other boiled sugar over this; give it one boil, remove it from the fire, and add two or three table-spoonfuls of sherry.

PUDDINGS AND CUSTARDS.

Plum-pudding, with Rum or Brandy (*Gouffé*).

Take three-quarters of a pound of chopped suet, three-quarters of a pound of stoned raisins, three-quarters of a pound of currants, quarter of a pound of citron, three-quarters of a pound of sugar, three-quarters of a pound of bread-crumbs, two apples cut into small dice, and the grated peel of a lemon; mix the whole in a basin, with three pounded cloves, a pinch of salt, six eggs, and half a gill of rum or brandy. Butter a pudding-mold, fill it with the mixture, and tie a cloth over the top. Place a plate at the bottom of a kettle which is three-parts full of boiling water. Put the pudding in, and boil for four hours, keeping the pot replenished with boiling water. Turn out the pudding on a hot dish; sprinkle over it sugar. Pour over half a pint of warm rum or brandy, and light it when putting the pudding on the table.

German Sauce.—Made with eight yolks of eggs, quarter of a pound of sugar, three gills of Madeira, and the grated peel of half a lemon. Stir it over the fire until the spoon is coated. Serve in a boat. Or serve a common brandy sauce, or the same kind of sauce flavored with rum, if rum should be used in the pudding.

Plum-pudding (*Mrs. General Sherman*).

Ingredients: One cupful of butter, one cupful of sugar, half a cupful of cream, half a cupful of rum, one cupful of ale, one cupful of suet (chopped), one cupful of fruit (currants and raisins), half a cupful of candied orange cut fine, six eggs well beaten, two grated nutmegs, one tea-spoonful of ground cinnamon, half a tea-spoonful of ground cloves, bread-crumbs.

Beat the butter and sugar together to a cream. The bread-crumbs should be dried thoroughly, and passed through a sieve. Beat all well together before adding the bread-crumbs, then add enough of them to give proper consistency. Put the pudding into a tin mold (not quite filling it), and boil it four hours.

The Sauce.—Use equal quantities of butter and sugar. Cream the butter, then add the sugar, beating them both until very light. Add then the beaten yolk of an egg, and a little grated nutmeg. Heat on the fire a large wine-glassful of sherry wine diluted with the same quantity of water, and when just beginning to boil, stir it into the butter and sugar.

Pudding with Remains of Plum-pudding.

Line a *charlotte* mold or basin with slices of cold plum-pudding, cut so that they will fit closely together. Fill the inside with a sufficient quantity of gelatine pudding   Set it in a cool place to stiffen. Turn out the *charlotte* on a dish, with a brandy sauce on the bottom.

Plainer Fruit Pudding.

Ingredients: One cupful of sugar, one-quarter of a pound of raisins, one cupful of butter, one half-pound of English currants, three and a half cupfuls of flour, a little citron sliced, four eggs, the whites and yolks beaten separately. Put one tea-spoonful of saleratus with, one half-cupful of cream. Flour the raisins, currants, and citron before adding to the mixture.

Boil it three hours in a floured cloth, or in buttered forms, large or small. Pour some brandy on top, and set it on fire just before taking to the dining-room. Serve with brandy-sauce.

Suet-pudding (*Mrs. Gratz Brown*).

Ingredients: One cupful of suet chopped fine, one cupful of molasses, one cupful of sweet milk, one cupful of raisins, one tea-spoonful of salt, one small tea-spoonful of soda mixed in the molasses, three and a half cupfuls of flour.

Boil in a bag or form three hours; or, better, steam it. It may be steamed in tea-cups, filling them a little more than half full. Serve with brandy-sauce.

Prune-pudding (*Grace Greenwood*).

This is the same as the suet-pudding, excepting that one half-pound of prunes and one half-pound of English currants are substituted for the raisins.

Eve's Pudding (*Mrs. Frank Blair*).

Ingredients: Six ounces of bread-crumbs, six ounces of sugar, six ounces of raisins or currants, six ounces of butter cut in small pieces, or beef suet chopped fine, six large apples chopped, one table-spoonful of flour, six eggs, one table-spoonful of cinnamon, one tea-spoonful of ground cloves.

Flour the fruit. Mix eggs and sugar together, and the suet and apples; then mix all, adding the beaten whites of the eggs the last thing. Boil it in a form or bag three hours, or bake it two hours. Serve with brandy-sauce.

A Spiced Apple-pudding.

Ingredients: Three tea-cupfuls of bread-crumbs, three tea-cupfuls of apples chopped, one tea-cupful of sugar, one-quarter of a pound of raisins, perhaps a little citron, two table-spoonfuls of brandy, one table-spoonful of ground cinnamon, half a tea-spoonful of ground cloves, one tea-spoonful of mace, two or three eggs beaten separately.

Cook the bread-crumbs a few minutes with a pint of milk before adding the other ingredients; add the whites of the eggs the last thing before baking. Bake half an hour, if the oven is quite hot. Serve with any sweet sauce.

Cottage-pudding.

Ingredients: One cupful of sugar, one and one-half cupfuls of flour, one table-spoonful of butter, one half-cupful of milk, two eggs beaten separately, one tea-spoonful of baking-powder, or one half-tea-spoonful of soda, and one tea-spoonful of cream of tartar. Brandy or wine sauce.

Minute-pudding.

Ingredients: One quart of milk, salt, two eggs, about a pint of flour.

Beat the eggs well; add the flour and enough milk to make it smooth. Butter the saucepan, and put in the remainder of the milk well salted; when it boils, stir in the flour, eggs, etc., lightly; let it cook well. It should be of the consistency of thick corn mush. Serve immediately with the following simple sauce, viz., milk sweetened to taste, and flavored with grated nutmeg.

Nantucket Berry-pudding.

Ingredients: One pint of grated cold boiled potatoes, one pint of flour, one quarter of a pound of butter, one tea-spoonful of salt, and almost any kind of berries.

Wet these with milk or water to the consistency of soft biscuit-dough; roll it; spread with blackberries, raspberries, cherries, or stewed dry berries. Roll, fasten in a cloth, and steam it an hour and a quarter. Serve with any sweet pudding-sauce.

Gelatine-pudding (*Miss Colby, of Rochester*).

Separate the whites and yolks of four eggs. With the yolks make a boiled custard (with a pint of milk, and sugar to taste). Set a third of a box of gelatine to soak a few minutes in a little cold water, then dissolve it with three-fourths of a cupful of boiling water. When the custard has cooled, add the gelatine water and the whites of the eggs beaten to a stiff froth; flavor with vanilla, stir all together, and put it into a mold or molds. It will settle into three layers, and is a very pretty pudding, tasting much like a *charlotte-russe*. A pretty effect can be obtained by using Coxe's *pink* gelatine.

Tapioca-pudding.

Pare and core (with a tube) six or seven apples; lay them in a buttered dish. Pour over a cupful of tapioca or sago one quart of boiling water; let it stand an hour; add two tea-cupfuls of sugar, a little lemon, vanilla, or wine; pour this over the apples, and bake an hour. Peaches (fresh or canned) may be substituted, and are an improvement.

Tapioca Cream.

Soak a tea-cupful of tapioca overnight in milk. The next day, stir into it the yolks of three eggs well beaten and a cupful of sugar. Place a quart of milk on the fire, let it come to the boiling-point, and then stir in the tapioca, and let the whole cook until it has thickened; then take it off the fire, and stir in the whites of the eggs beaten to a froth. Flavor to taste. A small portion of the beaten whites of the eggs can be saved to decorate the top. Stir into the latter a little sugar, put it into a paper funnel, press it out over the top of the pudding according to fancy, and place it in the oven a few moments to color.

CABINET-PUDDING (*Mrs. Pope*).

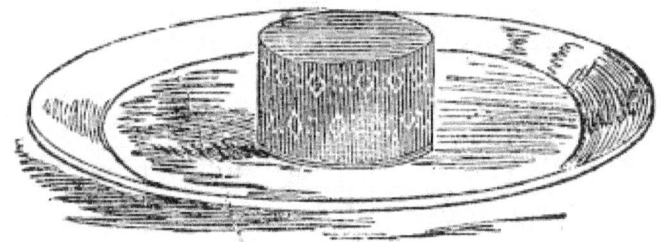

Butter a mold well; line the bottom with raisins and with citron cut into fancy shapes; cover this with pieces of cake, then more raisins and citron, alternating with the cake, until the mold is full to within an inch and a half of the top. Mix in a bowl three table-spoonfuls of sugar and the yolks of three eggs until they are a cream; then mix in slowly a pint of milk just brought to the boiling-point. Pour this over the cake, etc., in the mold. Put this into a pan of cold water, so that the water may cover one-third of the mold. Set it over the fire until the water boils; then put the whole into the oven to bake an hour. Serve with wine-sauce.

BATTER-PUDDINGS BAKED.

Ingredients: One quart of sifted flour, butter the size of an egg, one pint of milk, half a tea-spoonful of salt, four eggs.

Scald the milk, and melt the butter in it. When partly cooled, stir in the yolks of the eggs well beaten, then the salt and flour. When quite cold, stir in lightly the whites of the eggs beaten to a stiff froth. Bake in rather large patty-pans. Serve immediately with a sauce. The puddings should be light puffs. Strawberry-sauce is especially nice with these puddings.

ROLY-POLY PUDDING BOILED.

Make a biscuit-dough and roll it out into a square about a fourth of an inch thick. Spread over it (leaving an inch uncovered at the edges) almost any kind of fruit, or berries, such as strawberries, raspberries, etc., sweetened, or preserves. Roll it tight. Sew it in a cloth, giving room for it to swell. Boil or steam it an hour. Serve with almost any kind of pudding sauce. A nice roly-poly pudding may be made with sponge-cake baked in sheets, spread with preserves or jelly, rolled, sprinkled on top with sugar, and served with wine-sauce.

BAKED BERRY ROLLS.

Roll biscuit-dough thin, in the form of a large square, or into small squares. Spread over with berries. Roll the crust, and put the rolls into a dripping-pan close together until full; then put into the pan water, sugar, and pieces of butter. Bake them. Serve any of the pudding sauces.

SWEDISH PUDDING.

Ingredients: One half-pound of flour, one half-pound of butter, half-pound of sugar, eight eggs, a little salt.

Rub the sugar and butter to a cream; add the yolks well beaten, the salt, flour, and, lastly, the whites of the eggs beaten to a stiff froth. Put the batter three-fourths of an inch deep into tea-cups. Cook by steaming them in a steamer about half an hour. The batter will fill the cups. Turn them out on a hot platter. Serve immediately with a clear brandy-sauce in the bottom of the dish. Half the above amount will be sufficient for a small family.

CHERRY-PUDDING (*Mrs. Bonner*).

Ingredients: Two eggs, one cupful of sweet milk, three tea-spoonfuls of yeast powder, flour to make a stiff batter, as many cherries or fruit of any kind as can be stirred in.

Boil or steam it two hours. Serve with fruit sauce, made as in receipt for "fruit sauces" of the same kind of fruit of which the pudding is made.

A CORN-STARCH PUDDING.

Many kinds of puddings can be made with this receipt by adding different flavorings. I consider it a great success; besides, it is very easily and quickly made. It may or may not be served with a boiled custard made with the yolks of the eggs.

Ingredients: One pint of rich milk, two table-spoonfuls of corn starch, a scant half-cupful of sugar, whites of three or four eggs, a little salt, flavoring.

Beat the eggs to a stiff froth. Dissolve the corn starch in a little of the milk. Stir the sugar into the remainder of the milk, which place on the fire. When it begins to boil, add the dissolved corn starch. Stir constantly for a few moments, when it will become a smooth paste; now stir in the beaten whites of the eggs, and let it remain a little longer to cook the eggs. It can be flavored with vanilla, and put into a form; yet it is still better as a

Cocoa-nut Pudding.

When the preceding pudding is just finished, add half a cocoa-nut grated; put it into a mold. Serve with whipped-cream around it, or a sauce of boiled custard made with the yolks of the eggs. As only half of a cocoa-nut is used for this pudding, sprinkle sugar on the other half, and spread it on something, when it will keep a month. In that time perhaps another pudding of the same kind may be wanted. Fresh cocoa-nut is better and cheaper than the desiccated cocoa-nut. It requires the whole of a twenty-five cent package of the desiccated cocoa-nut, and only half of a fresh one, which costs but ten cents.

Chocolate-pudding.

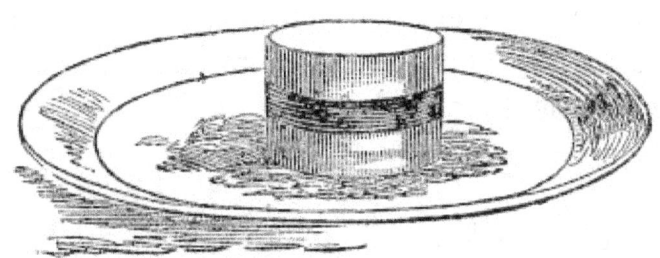

With still the same receipt for a corn-starch pudding, first flavor the whole with vanilla; now take out a third of the pudding; flavor the remainder in the kettle with a bar of chocolate, softened, mashed, and dissolved with a little milk. Put half of the chocolate-pudding in the bottom of a mold (which has been wet in cold water); smooth the top; next make a layer with the white pudding (the third taken out); smooth it also; next the remainder of the chocolate-pudding. Serve with whipped cream, or a boiled custard made with the yolks of the eggs and flavored with vanilla, around it; or, the one-third portion of pudding may be flavored with half a bar of chocolate, and placed in the centre of the two layers of white, as in the picture; or one can use the same receipt for a corn-starch pudding, and flavor it with chopped pine-apple, strawberries, or, in winter, with dried cherries swollen in water; or it may be flavored with chocolate, with the white centre part of cocoa-nut.

Cocoa-nut Puddings, in Paper Cases.

Melt over the fire butter the size of an egg, with a cupful of sugar, and a table-spoonful of water. Pour them into a dish when they have boiled a couple of minutes, and let them cool; mix with them half of a cocoa-nut grated, a table-spoonful of small cuts of citron, the grated rind and juice of half a lemon, and the yolks of four eggs beaten separately; add the whites (beaten to a stiff froth) the last thing. Fill little paper cases (see page 6), and bake immediately. They may be served hot or cold. Of course it may all be baked in one dish; but it makes a very dainty course to serve one of these cases placed on a plate for each person.

Egg Soufflé, in Paper Cases.

Make a boiled custard of cream with half a pint of milk, yolks of two eggs, three table-spoonfuls of sugar, a heaping tea-spoonful of flour, a very little butter, salt, and a flavoring of vanilla, or any thing else, as preferred. When it has just thickened a little, take it off the fire, and let it partly cool. Add then two raw yolks of eggs and four whites beaten to a stiff froth. Butter the paper cases, fill them with this preparation, and bake them ten or fifteen minutes in a moderate oven.

Snow-pudding (*Miss Amelia Foote*).

Cover one-third of a package of gelatine with a little cold water, and, when softened, stir into it a pint of boiling water; add one cupful of sugar, or sugar to taste, and either the juice of two lemons, or half a tea-cupful of wine: when cold, and beginning to thicken, add the well-beaten whites of three eggs. Beat all lightly and smoothly together, pour the mixture into a mold, and set it away until hard. Serve in the centre of a platter, with a boiled custard poured around, made with the yolks of three eggs, one pint of milk, and half a cupful of sugar.

Boiled Custard (No. 1).

I will venture a receipt for boiled custard (perhaps it should be granted that every one knows how to make it), as it is so often used in making many kinds of dessert, and as an excellent sauce for several puddings.

It is considered better made of the yolks only of the eggs (some whites may be used, however). A dessert-spoonful of sugar is enough for each egg, and five yolks are quite sufficient for a quart of milk. Beat the yolks and the sugar together to a froth, and stir in the milk; put it into a custard-boiler, or, if one has none, into a small tin pail. Place this in a kettle of boiling water; stir the mixture constantly until it is a little thickened. If it is well stirred, the custard will be a smooth cream; if allowed to remain a few moments too long in the boiling water after it begins to thicken, it will curdle and be spoiled. Do not flavor it with any of the essences, wines, or brandy, until after it is cooked; if either a vanilla-bean or peach-leaves are used, cook them with the custard.

If the whole eggs are preferred, for economy's sake, to be used (and they make very good custard), allow four eggs to a quart of milk, and four dessert-spoonfuls of sugar. If the milk is first boiled before it is added to the other ingredients, there will be less danger of the custard curdling.

BOILED CUSTARD (*Miss Eliza Brown*), No. 2.

Beat the yolks of three eggs very lightly; stir into them two small table-spoonfuls of corn starch, dissolved in a little milk, and one tea-cupful of sugar. Bring two quarts of milk to a boil, then take it off the fire; pour it into the eggs, etc., a little at first; return it to the fire, and stir it until it thickens, not allowing it to boil; let it remain long enough to well cook the starch. Now stir in lightly the whites of four eggs beaten to a stiff froth, allowing the custard to remain a half-minute on the fire to set the eggs. Flavor with vanilla or chocolate, or with both.

APPLE MÉRINGUE (*Mrs. Shaw*).

Boil tart apples after they are pared and cored; rub the pulp through a colander, and sweeten it to taste. To a pint of the soft pulp stir in lightly the whites of three eggs, beaten to a stiff froth. Flavor with grated rind and juice of lemon, or with lemon or vanilla extract. Serve it with cream. It is a decided improvement to put this into a pudding-dish and cover it with the beaten whites of two or three eggs, sweetened and flavored. Color it in the oven. Serve with cream or custard.

BAKED APPLES.

Pare and core large, juicy pippins, without cutting them to pieces; fill the cavities with sugar, and a little lemon-juice or extract, and some thin slices of the yellow part of the lemon-rind; put them into a pan with a little water in the bottom; sprinkle sugar over the tops, baste them often, and, when done, set them away to cool. Serve them with cream, or they may be served with whipped cream, flavored with sugar and essence of lemon, poured over so as to nearly conceal them; or serve them with a boiled custard poured over them.

FRIAR'S OMELET (*Mrs. Treat*).

Stew six or seven good-sized apples as for apple-sauce; stir in, when cooked and still warm, butter the size of a pigeon's egg, and one cupful of sugar; when cold, stir in three well-beaten eggs and a little lemon-juice. Now put a small piece of butter into a sauté pan, and when hot throw in a cupful of bread-crumbs; stir them over the fire until they assume a light-brown color. Butter a mold, and sprinkle on the bottom and sides as many of these bread-crumbs as will adhere; fill in the apple preparation, sprinkle bread-crumbs on top, bake it for fifteen or twenty minutes, and turn it out on a good-sized platter. It can be eaten with or without a sweet sauce.

Floating Islands.

Separate the whites and yolks of four eggs; with the yolks make a boiled custard with, say, a large pint of milk, four table-spoonfuls of sugar, and a flavoring of vanilla, essence of lemon, sherry-wine, peach-leaves, or any of the usual flavorings. Beat the whites to a stiff froth, sweetening and flavoring them a little also. Wet a long spoon, turn it around in the beaten egg, taking out a piece of oblong shape; poach it, turning it around in boiling water, or milk, which is better. When the custard is cold, pour it into a glass dish, and place these poached whites on top; or make a circle of the whites in a platter, and pour the custard between.

Tipsy-pudding.

Soak a sponge-cake baked in a form (or, in fact, dry pieces of cake of any kind can be used) in sherry-wine. When saturated enough, so that it will not fall to pieces, pour over it a boiled custard (No. 1), flavored with any thing preferred. If placed in a glass dish, decorate with the beaten whites of the eggs poached, and with dots of jelly. If served in a common platter, squeeze the beaten whites (sweetened and flavored) through a funnel in any fancy shapes over the pudding, and put it into the oven to receive a delicate color.

Lemon-pudding.

Beat the yolks of two eggs in a pudding-dish; add two cupfuls of sugar. Dissolve four table-spoonfuls of corn starch in a little cold water. Stir into it two tea-cupfuls of boiling water. Put in the juice of two lemons, with some of the grated peel. Mix all together with a tea-spoonful of butter. Bake it about fifteen minutes. When done, spread over the top the beaten whites of the eggs sweetened, and let it color a moment in the oven. To be eaten hot or cold.

Blanc-mange.

Put half a paper of gelatine, two ounces of sugar, half of the very thin rind of a lemon, and eight bitter almonds, blanched and bruised, into a pint of milk, and let it stand an hour. Place it over the fire, and let it come merely to the scalding-point, stirring it well to dissolve the gelatine.

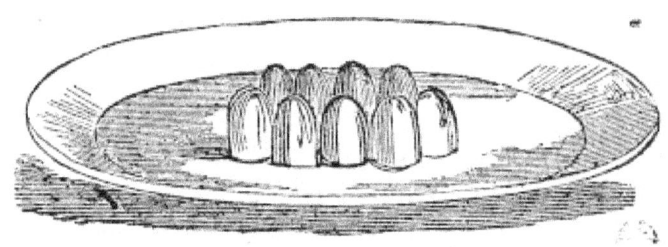

Strain it into a bowl, add a pint of cream, and a little wine or brandy, to taste. Stir it occasionally, to prevent the cream from settling on the surface. Turn it, avoiding the settlings, into molds, to harden; or, in place of almonds, a stick of cinnamon may be substituted; or infuse a few more almonds, and omit the wine or brandy; or, the blanc-mange may be flavored with maraschino, or any other liqueur. I prefer blanc-mange made with corn starch, as the same ingredients necessary for a blanc-mange proper are better made into Bavarian creams.

Corn-starch Pudding.

Ingredients: One and one-half pints of rich milk, one large heaping table-spoonful of corn starch, one scant cupful of sugar, four eggs, omitting two whites, a little salt, and flavoring.

Bring the milk and the sugar almost to a boil, then add the corn starch (stirred smooth with a little milk), and a pinch of salt. Stir it at the back of the range for five minutes, not allowing it to boil. Then take it off the fire; when a little cooled, stir in the eggs, and when well and smoothly mixed, place the kettle again on the fire for only a few moments, to be sure that the eggs are slightly cooked. Now stir in the flavoring, if it is an extract. Zest (sugar rubbed on fresh lemon-peel) is an exceedingly delicate flavoring. The vanilla powder boiled in the milk is better than the extract.

It makes a pretty dish to pour this into cups or little molds, and, when cold and solid, to arrange them in a circle or, according to taste, on a platter, with strawberry, grape, or any kind of fruit sauce, or whipped cream poured into the bottom of the dish; or, mold it in a circular form, and pile up any kind of berries in the centre, with or without whipped cream. For an invalid I prefer the other receipt for "a corn-starch pudding."

The common rule for corn-starch pudding is one quart of milk, three eggs, three table-spoonfuls of corn starch, one even cupful of sugar; add flavoring and a little salt.

Bread-pudding.

Soak some crumbled bread in milk. Put a layer of this (rather moist) in the bottom of a pudding-dish; sprinkle over some raisins and a little cinnamon powder, then another layer of soaked bread-crumbs, raisins, and cinnamon powder. Now beat up three eggs (to about a quart of soaked bread-crumbs) with two heaping table-spoonfuls of sugar; mix into it a quarter of a cupful of rum, brandy, or wine, and pour it all over the pudding in the dish. Bake about twenty minutes.

Bread-and-butter Pudding.

Strew layers of English currants between slices of buttered bread (crust cut off). Pour over them a boiled custard flavored with nutmeg or any other flavoring desired. Set them into the oven to soak, and bake about fifteen minutes.

Fried Bread-pudding.

Cut the crust from slices of bread. Cut them into pieces of the same shape and size. Soak them a few moments in custard—*i.e.*, some milk, one or two eggs, and sugar to taste, and a flavoring of cinnamon. *Sauté* them in hot lard to a delicate brown. Serve with brandy-sauce, or almost any kind of sweet sauce.

Indian-corn Pudding.

Scald a quart of milk, and stir in seven table-spoonfuls of sifted corn-meal, a tea-spoonful of salt, one tea-cupful of molasses, a table-spoonful of ginger. Bake three hours.

BAVARIAN CREAMS.

There is not a more delicious dessert than that of Bavarian cream. These creams are exceedingly easy to make, and, as they are prepared some time before dinner, they have the advantage of being out of the way when cooking this meal. They are a cheap country dessert, where one has plenty of cream, yet are not so very expensive in the city, as it only requires a pint of common cream to make a quart and a half of Bavarian cream.

When cream is thoroughly chilled, it is much more readily whipped. A pint can be whipped in a few minutes with a little tin tube cream-whipper. If no whipper is at hand, beat the cream with a fork, and skim off the whipped cream as it rises. It is always better not to cook gelatine; it should be soaked in a little water near the fire for an hour or two, when it will be entirely dissolved, and then it should be stirred into the custard while it is still hot. In making the Bavarian creams, do not add the whipped cream to the ingredients with the gelatine until they are quite cold and are beginning to set, or they would otherwise dissolve the cream. The ingredients will set very soon if placed on ice. The pine-apple Bavarian is especially nice, and can be made with the canned pine-apple if the fresh pine-apple can not be obtained; however, there is not much choice, as they are all delicious.

The Bavarian creams all make good *charlottes-russe*, the peach Bavarian making an especially delicious one. Sometimes these mixtures are frozen, and put into *charlotte* molds; the cake is formed in molds a trifle larger. When the cream is frozen, it is inserted into the cake just before serving. When freezing the mixture, the whipped cream is not added until the custard or ingredients with the gelatine are partly frozen.

Bavarian Cream, with Vanilla (*Mrs. Blair*).

Whip one pint of cream to a stiff froth, laying it on a sieve. Boil another pint of cream or rich milk, with a vanilla bean, and two table-spoonfuls of sugar, until it is well flavored; then take it off the fire and add half a box of Nelson's or Coxe's gelatine soaked for an hour in half a cupful of water, in a warm place near the range; when slightly cooled, stir in the yolks of four eggs well beaten. When it has become quite cold, and begins to thicken, stir it without ceasing a few minutes until it is very smooth, then stir in the whipped cream lightly until it is well mixed. Put it into a mold or molds, and set it on ice, or in some cool place.

BAVARIAN CREAM, WITH CHOCOLATE,

is made as the preceding cream, adding two sticks of chocolate, soaked and smoothed, to the yolks of the eggs.

BAVARIAN CREAM, WITH STRAWBERRIES.

After picking two pounds and a half of strawberries, squeeze them through a colander, and add six ounces of sugar to the juice; when the sugar is dissolved, add half a box of gelatine soaked as before described. Place it on the ice, stir it smooth when it begins to set, then stir in a pint of cream whipped; put it into a mold or molds, and serve with fresh strawberries around it.

BAVARIAN CREAM, WITH ALMONDS.

Take three ounces of sweet and one ounce of bitter almonds, blanch and skin them, and put them into a pan on a moderate fire, stirring them continually. As soon as they have acquired a fine yellow color, take them off the fire, and when cold pound them into fine pieces. Then add a pint of cream or rich milk (nearly boiling), and two or three table-spoonfuls of sugar, and half a package of gelatine, which has been soaked as before described. Put it upon the ice, and when about to thicken stir it until it is very smooth, then stir in lightly a pint of cream whipped, and put it into a mold.

BAVARIAN CREAM, WITH PEACHES.

Cut eighteen fine peaches into small pieces, and boil them with half a pound of sugar. When they are reduced to a marmalade, squeeze them through a sieve or colander. Then add half a package of dissolved gelatine, and a glassful of good cream. Stir it well, to make it smooth when it is about to set, then add the pint of cream whipped, and mold it. It makes a still prettier dish to serve halves or quarters of fresh peaches half frozen, around the cream.

Bavarian Cream, with Pine-apple.

Cut a pine-apple into fine pieces; boil it with one half-pound, or a coffee-cupful of sugar; pass the marmalade through a sieve or colander; turn off part of the juice; add half a package of dissolved gelatine. Stir, and add the pint of cream whipped, as before described. Mold it.

Bavarian Cream, with Coffee.

Throw three heaping table-spoonfuls of fresh roasted and ground Mocha coffee into a pint of boiling rich milk. Make a strong infusion, strain it, and add to it the whipped yolks of four eggs well beaten, with an even cupful of sugar. Stir the custard over the fire until it begins to thicken; take it off the fire, and add to it, while still hot, half a box of gelatine which has been standing an hour on the hearth to dissolve in a little cold water. When just beginning to set, stir it well to make it smooth, then add the pint of cream whipped. Mold it.

Charlotte-russe.

The sponge-cake may be made with four eggs, one cupful of sugar, one and one-half cupfuls of flour, and two even tea-spoonfuls of yeast powder, or as described for sponge jelly-cake

To make an even sheet, professional cooks pass the cake batter through the *méringue* bag on a large sheet of foolscap paper in rows which touch each other, and which run together smoothly when baking; or, without the *méringue* bag, it may be spread over the sheet as evenly as possible. When baked, an oval piece is cut to fit the bottom of the *charlotte* pan, then even-sized parallelograms are cut to fit around the sides. Fill with cream made as follows: Whip one pint of cream flavored with vanilla to a stiff froth, and add to it the well-beaten whites of two eggs, and one half-pound of pulverized sugar; mix it all lightly and carefully together. Fill the *charlotte* pan, or pans, and put them into the ice-chest to set.

This is the best and simplest manner of making a *charlotte-russe*. Many take the trouble to add gelatine, which is unnecessary. Professor Blot made the filling of his *charlotte-russe* of sweetened and flavored whipped cream only. It will harden without difficulty if placed upon the ice, and it is very delicate; yet the whites of eggs are an improvement. If there is only enough cake at hand to fit the sides of the pan, put a paper in the bottom of the mold cut to fit it, and the *charlotte* can be served without a top.

These *charlottes* are very prettily decorated on top with icing squeezed through a small-sized funnel; or, you may pour a transparent icing over the whole, and make the decoration over this with the common icing. Sometimes they are made in little molds, one *charlotte* for each plate, and, again, a large *charlotte* is decorated with a circle of strawberries around it.

Cream is much more easily frothed when placed on ice and thoroughly chilled before whipping; when whipping it, place the froth on a sieve, and all that drops through can be returned to the bowl to be rewhipped. Sometimes professional cooks work the froth with an egg-whisk to make it finer grained.

Ambrosia.

Slice peeled oranges. Make alternate layers of orange slices, sugar, and grated cocoa-nut, until a glass dish is filled, having grated cocoa-nut on top; now pour a little sherry wine over the top, to run through the mixtures. It is as often served without the wine.

DESSERTS OF RICE.

To Boil Rice.

Always cook rice with plenty of salt; it is insipid without it. It is sometimes cooked in a steamer, with milk, without stirring it; although it is more quickly cooked by soaking it an hour or two, and then throwing it into salted boiling water in the brightest of saucepans. To half a pound of the rice use about five pints of water. Let it simmer about twenty minutes. Handle it carefully, not to break the kernels.

Rice-pudding.

This receipt makes one of the plainest and best puddings ever eaten. It is a success where every grain of rice seems lying in a creamy bed.

Ingredients: One cupful of boiled rice (better if just cooked, and still hot), three cupfuls of milk, three-quarters of a cupful of sugar, a tablespoonful of corn starch, two eggs; add flavoring.

Dissolve the corn starch first with a little milk, and then stir in the remainder of the milk; add the yolks of the eggs and the sugar beaten together. Now put this over the fire (there is less risk of burning in a custard-kettle), and when hot add the hot rice. It will seem as if there were too much milk for the rice; but there is not. Stir it carefully until it begins to thicken like boiled custard, then take it off the fire, and add the flavoring, say, extract of lemon. Put it into a pudding-dish, and place it in the oven. Now beat the whites of the eggs to a stiff froth, and add a little sugar and flavoring. Take the pudding from the oven when colored a little, spread the froth over the top, and return it to the oven for a few minutes to give the froth a delicate coloring.

Rice-cones.

Mold boiled rice, when hot, in cups which have been previously dipped in cold water; when cold, turn them out on a flat dish, arranging them uniformly; then with a tea-spoon scoop out a little of the rice from the top of each cone, and put in its place any kind of jelly. Just before serving, pour in the bottom of the dish hot brandy-sauce. For a change, it is well to boil a stick of cinnamon in the rice to flavor it.

Rice-cake, with Peaches.

When some rice is cooked in a steamer with milk, and is still hot, add a little butter, sugar, and one or two eggs. Butter a plain pudding-mold, strew the butter with bread-crumbs, and put in a layer of rice half an inch thick; then a layer of peaches, and continue alternate layers of each until the mold is full. Bake this for about fifteen or twenty minutes in an oven; when done, turn the cake out of the mold, and pour in the bottom of the dish a boiled custard-sauce flavored with wine, or any thing preferred.

Rice-cake, with Pine-apple.

Prepare rice as above. Cut the pine-apple into dice, and boil them in sirup (water and sugar boiled ten or fifteen minutes); drain and mix them in the rice. Butter a plain pudding-mold or basin, and strew it with bread-crumbs; put in the rice and pine-apple, and bake it; when done, turn it out of the mold, and pour around it a sauce made as follows: Peel three large apples, and cook them in one pint of sirup sweetened to taste. When the apples are quite soft, strain them through a sieve, and mix this sirup with that in which the pine-apple was cooked; boil, or reduce it until it coats the spoon.

Ground Rice-pudding, with Chocolate Sauce.

Steam one quarter of a pound of ground rice and one pint of cream a quarter of an hour, then flavor it with vanilla; add one ounce of butter, the yolks of four eggs, let it cool, and beat it for half an hour; beat up the whites of the eggs to a froth, which mix in gently. Steam it a quarter of an hour. Serve it with half a pint of boiled custard, having one ounce of soaked and mashed chocolate stirred well into it, poured into the bottom of the dish.

Orange Snow-balls (*Mrs. Acton*).

Boil some rice for ten minutes, drain, and let it cool. Pare some oranges, taking off all the thick white skin; spread the rice in as many portions as there are oranges, on some pudding or dumpling cloths. Tie the fruit (surrounded by the rice) separately in these, and boil the balls for an hour; turn them carefully on a dish, sprinkle over plenty of sifted sugar. Serve with any kind of sauce or sweetened cream.

Apple Snow-balls.

Pare and core some large apples without dividing them. Prepare the rice as in the foregoing receipt; inclose the apples separately in it, and boil them three-quarters of an hour.

Sauce.—A little butter and sugar mixed to a cream; a spoonful of corn starch cooked in two cupfuls of boiling water; flavoring of cinnamon. To mix, see Sweet Sauces.

Rice Soufflé.

Ingredients: Half a cupful of rice, one even cupful of sugar, one pint of milk, butter the size of a butter-nut, half a lemon, five eggs.

Throw the rice into boiling salted water, and let it boil for ten minutes. Then put it into a stew-pan with the milk, butter and sugar, and set this to simmer very slowly for about half an hour, when the rice should be very soft (or the pan can be placed in a vessel of boiling water, or in a steamer). If it is placed directly on the range, much care should be taken not to let it burn. Now work the rice, etc., with a wooden spoon until it is a smooth paste; add the yolks of the eggs beaten to a perfect froth, and a lump of loaf sugar (mashed) which has absorbed all the oil out of the rind of the whole lemon (called zest); add also the juice of half of the lemon. If the rice is now too firm, add a little cream also. When cold, stir into this the whites of the eggs beaten to the stiffest possible froth, and put the mixture into a flat pudding-dish, or into little paper cases (see page 61). Sprinkle granulated sugar over the top or tops. Bake in the oven about ten minutes. Serve immediately, or the *soufflé* will fall. Ground rice may be used instead of whole rice. It should be rubbed smooth with a little cold milk, and then added to the remainder of the milk and the butter on the fire, and stirred until it thickens. It is then taken off the fire, sweetened, and flavored; the beaten yolks and then the beaten whites are stirred in quickly, and the sugar is sprinkled over the top, when all is put into the oven.

Rice Croquettes.

Ingredients: To half a pound of rice, one quart of milk, one tea-cupful of sugar, a very little butter, yolks of one or two eggs beaten, flavoring, and a little salt.

Soak the rice three or four hours in water; drain, and put into a basin with the milk and salt. Set the basin in the steamer, and cook until thoroughly done. Then stir in carefully the sugar, the yolks of one or two eggs, very little butter, and flavor with extract of lemon or vanilla. If fresh lemon is used, add a little zest. When cool enough to handle, form into small balls; press the thumb into the centre of each; insert a little marmalade, or jelly of any kind, and close the rice well over them. Roll in beaten eggs (sweetened a little), and bread-crumbs. Fry in boiling-hot lard.

Rice Pancakes, with Preserves.

Make the pancakes (see page 70), and while hot spread them with butter, and with almost any kind of preserve or jelly; roll them, cut off the ends, arrange them tastefully on a hot platter, sprinkle sugar over the tops, and serve immediately.

WINE JELLIES.

Wine Jelly.

Ingredients: One box of gelatine soaked in one pint of clear cold water, one pint of wine, the juice and the thin cuts of rinds of three lemons, one and three-quarter pounds of loaf-sugar, one quart of clear boiling water, the whites of two eggs (well beaten) and the shells, with a small stick of cinnamon.

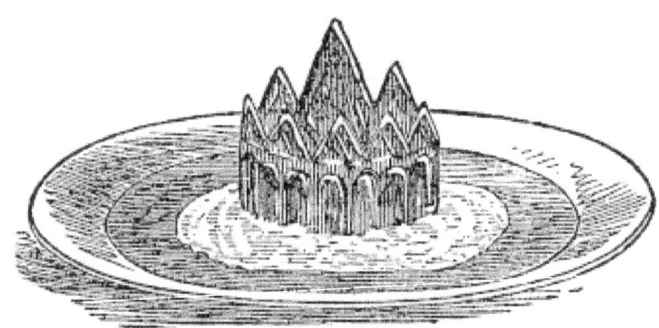

Soak the gelatine in the pint of cold water an hour, then pour over it the quart of boiling water, stirring it well; now add the wine, sugar, eggs, lemon-juice (strained in a fine strainer), and the thinnest possible cuts from the peels of the lemons. These cuts take only the little globules of oil in the peel, which are exceedingly delicate in flavor, the white part being bitter. Add also the small stick of cinnamon, as it adds much to the flavor of the jelly. Put this into a porcelain kettle, let it boil rapidly about a quarter of a minute without stirring it; now, setting the kettle on the hearth, let it remain another half-minute to settle, then skim off carefully the scum which is at the top; pour it through the jelly-bag. It should be entirely clear: if, however, the first should not be so, return it to the bag.

Cold water should be poured into the molds, then emptied just before using. Jelly hardens much quicker on ice, or in the coolest place to be found.

Dip the molds into warm water a moment, before taking out the jelly. If allowed to remain a moment too long, the jelly might dissolve a little, injuring the form.

Many kinds of wines and liquors may be used. The above receipt is well proportioned for sherry, Madeira, or port; a smaller proportion of brandy, maraschino, noyau, or of punch would make sufficient flavoring; a larger portion of Champagne might be used, as it is not so strong.

ORANGE JELLY (*molded with Quarters of Oranges*).

Ingredients: Eight oranges, two lemons, three-quarters of a box of gelatine soaked in half a pint of cold water, three-quarters of a pound of loaf-sugar, one pint of boiling water, beaten whites and shells of two eggs.

Rub the loaf-sugar on the peels of two oranges and one lemon; squeeze the juice from six or seven oranges and two lemons, and strain it. Take off the peel carefully from two oranges, leaving only the transparent skin surrounding the quarters, and separate all the sections without breaking them. Soak the gelatine half an hour in half a pint of water; boil the other pint of water and the sugar together, skimming all the time until no more scum rises; then put in the sections of oranges, and when they have boiled about a minute take them out, and put them one side. Pour this sirup over the soaked gelatine, adding the orange and lemon juice, the beaten whites and the shells of two eggs. Put it on the fire, and let it boil about a quarter of a minute without stirring; then, placing it at the side of the fire, skim off carefully all the scum at the top, and pass it through the jelly-bag. When half of the jelly is in the mold, put it on the ice, and let it set hard enough to hold the orange sections, which place in a circular row around the edge of the mold; then add enough more jelly to cover the sections; when this has hardened, pour over the remainder of the jelly, which should have been kept in a warm place to prevent it from hardening. All the sections of orange may be put in with the first half of the jelly, as they will rise to the top, although they will not hold their places evenly. Or, if time is valuable, mold the jelly without the sections, and save them to garnish the jelly on the dish.

LEMON JELLY.

Ingredients: Half a box of gelatine soaked in half a pint of water, juice of five large lemons, two cupfuls of loaf-sugar, or sugar to taste, beaten white and shell of an egg, one and a half pints of boiling water.

Soak the gelatine in the half-pint of water half an hour. Rub several of the pieces of the sugar on the peel of the lemon, to soak the oil on the surface. Pour a pint and a half of boiling water on the soaked gelatine, and add lemon-juice, sugar, and egg; let it come to a boil, then set it at the side of the range a few moments; skim carefully, and pass through the jelly-bag into molds.

Macedoine of Fruits.

This is made with any kind of jelly; however, jelly made with Champagne or sherry is preferable. Any of the delicate fruits of the season, such as grapes, cherries, peaches, strawberries, raspberries, mulberries, currants (on their stems), plums, and orange sections, or preserved fruits, such as brandied cherries, peaches, etc., are tastefully imbedded in the jelly, so as to show their forms and colors to best advantage. A fine bunch of Hamburg or of Malaga grapes is exceedingly pretty, incorporated whole into a clear Champagne jelly; it should be suspended with a small thread in the centre of the jelly-mold, and the jelly poured in when quite cold, although not set. The bunches of grapes are in this way much more easily imbedded than other fruits. In the latter case, the mold is placed on ice; a little jelly is poured in, and, when set, some fruits are arranged in a circle, or according to taste; more jelly poured in, and left to harden again; more fruit added, and thus continued until the mold is full.

Do not heat the jelly a second time; merely keep it in a warm place, awaiting that on the ice to harden.

Fancy Jellies.

Jelly is sometimes formed in a mold with a cylindrical tube in the centre; the open space in the centre is then filled with whipped cream. Then, to be still more fanciful, the whipped cream may be dotted with strawberries, or any kind of preserved fruits, such as cherries, grapes, cuts of peaches, etc., etc.

Then there is ribbon jelly, or jelly made in two colors, in this way: Half of a Champagne or sherry jelly is colored quite red with a few drops of prepared cochineal; a little pale jelly is poured into the mold, and, when set, a layer of the red jelly is poured carefully over it, and so continued until the mold is filled with alternate layers of the two colors.

Italian jelly is pretty also. The mold is half filled with jelly, and, when set, a chain of cakes of *blanc-mange* (made rather firm, hardened in a thin layer, and cut of equal sizes with a pepper-box cover or a small tin cutter) is arranged; then the remainder of the jelly is added to the mold.

Whipped jelly makes a pretty change. When it is set a little, put it into a bowl; whip it with an egg-whisk until it is full of air-bubbles. Fill the mold, and put on ice.

What To Do With Parts of Jelly Left Over in Winter.

Add lemon-juice; beat the jelly until it becomes entirely white, which will take some time, and put it into a mold again.

Calf's-foot Jelly.

I have made calf's-foot jelly twice, and never intend to make it again. I would not have made it the second time, except for the purpose of succeeding, and getting a reliable receipt for this book. At the first attempt, I happened to have company who had heard that I pretended to be a cook. The jelly was opaque, tasteless, and split in two. Here is a successful receipt. It requires almost every thing known in the cooking calender; but do not attempt it with less, and after a trial use gelatine only for jellies.

Ingredients: Four calf's feet boiled in a gallon of water, seven eggs, one and a half pounds of sugar, one pint of sherry wine, a stick of cinnamon, three cloves, and half a box of gelatine.

Split the calf's feet, break the bones, and place them on the fire at the back of the range, with a gallon of cold water, to boil gently for five hours. Skim the water often, which should be reduced to rather less than two quarts; then strain the jelly into a pan, and, when perfectly firm, remove the fat and sediment.

Add to the jelly the beaten whites and crushed shells of seven eggs, one and a half pounds of sugar, a pint of sherry wine, a stick of cinnamon, three cloves, and half a box of gelatine soaked in a little water, and whip this well together; set it over the fire, and when it has just begun to boil throw in the juice of six lemons, and one or two table-spoonfuls of clear, cold water; take the kettle off the fire, let it remain at the side in rather a hot place about ten minutes, then skim off carefully all the scum from the top. Put into the jelly-bag the thin cuts from the peels of four lemons, not cutting the white or under skin, as that is bitter; then pour in the jelly, having the apparatus near the fire to prevent the jelly hardening before it has all passed through.

CAKE.

Rules for Cake.—Have every thing ready before mixing the material—*i. e.*, the ingredients all measured and prepared, and the tins buttered. The sooner the cake is mixed (after the ingredients are ready) and put into the oven, the better. Sift the flour, and have it dry. Mix baking-powder or cream of tartar, if used, well into the flour, passing it through the sieve several times, if particular. Roll the sugar; mix sugar and butter together to a cream. The eggs must then be *very, very well* beaten separately. If one person makes the cake, beat the yolks first. If soda is used, dissolve it in the milk, or, if no milk is used, in a little lukewarm water; add it the last thing, unless fruit is used, when it should always be rolled in flour, and added the last thing. Cake, to be light, should be baked slowly at first, until the batter is evenly heated all through. Many leave the oven door slightly open for the first ten or fifteen minutes. The prepared flour is especially good for cake.

SPONGE-CAKE.

This is the most perfect of sponge-cakes, when properly made.

Ingredients: Ten eggs, one pound of *pulverized* sugar, half a pound of flour, juice of half a large lemon, with the rind grated.

After all the ingredients are quite ready—*i. e.*, the flour and sugar sifted, the lemon-peel grated, the half lemon squeezed, and the tins buttered—the success of this cake is in the beating of the eggs. Two persons should beat them at least half an hour, one beating the whites, and the other the yolks and half of the sugar together. Next cut the yolks into the whites, then stir in lightly the remainder of the sugar, then the flour and lemon by degrees.[J]

The oven heat should be rather *moderate* at first. Much of the success depends upon this, as the batter should be evenly heated throughout before it begins to rise. When baked, spread over the cakes a wafer thickness of icing

WHITE CAKE (*Miss Eliza Brown*).

I venture to say there is not to be found a better receipt for white cake than the following. The cake is mixed contrary to the usual rules for making cake, but it is the best mode for making it fine-grained and delicate.

Ingredients: Whites of six eggs, scant three-quarters of a cupful of butter, one and one-quarter cupfuls of pulverized sugar, two cupfuls of flour, juice of half a lemon, one-quarter of a tea-spoonful of soda.

If soda is used, mix it well with the flour, and pass it through the sieve several times to distribute it equally. Beat the butter to a light cream, and add the flour to it, stirring it in gradually with the ends of the fingers until it is a smooth paste. Beat the whites of the six eggs to a stiff froth, and mix in them the pulverized sugar; now stir the egg and sugar gradually into the flour and butter, adding also the lemon-juice, and mix it smoothly together with the egg-whisk. As soon as it is perfectly smooth, put it into the oven, the heat of which should be rather moderate at first. When done and still hot, spread over it a frosting made with the white of one egg, pulverized sugar (see page 304), and a flavoring of lemon. The frosting is a decided improvement, and, according to the receipt, only requires a few minutes to prepare.

This cake may be made with one tea-spoonful of baking-powder, or with prepared flour, or with the one-quarter tea-spoonful of soda and one-half tea-spoonful of cream of tartar, when the essence of lemon should be used instead of the lemon-juice.

JUMBLES (*Mrs. Wadsworth*).

Ingredients: Two cupfuls of sugar, three eggs (beaten separately); one cupful of butter, just enough flour to roll it out.

Mix quickly, and roll it thin. Cut out the cakes with a round cake-cutter, cutting them out again in the centre with the top of the pepper-glass of the caster. When they are in the pans, wet the tops, using a paste-brush or feather, with the white of an egg slightly beaten. Then sprinkle over very coarse-pounded lump-sugar; the sugar, in fact, in little lumps.

ALMOND JUMBLES.

Ingredients: One pound of sugar, one-half pound of butter, one pound of almonds blanched and chopped fine, two eggs, flour enough to mix stiff.

Roll thin. Moisten the top of each one with the white of eggs, and sprinkle with sugar. Bake quickly.

Some persons wet the jumbles with a brush or a little cloth saturated with sherry-wine after they are cooked, and then return them to the oven a few moments to dry.

Cocoa-nut Cake (*Miss Emma Witt, of Cleveland*).

Ingredients: One-half coffee-cupful of butter, two small tea-spoonfuls of cream of tartar, two and one-half coffee-cupfuls of sugar, one small tea-spoonful of soda, four and one-half coffee-cupfuls of flour, two grated cocoa-nuts, one coffee-cupful of sweet milk, the whites of seven eggs.

Reserve a large handful of the grated cocoa-nut to sprinkle on the frosting. This cake looks most beautiful mixed with fruit-cake in a cake-basket.

Fruit-cake (*Miss Abbie Carpenter, of Saratoga*).

Ingredients: One pound of flour, one pound of sugar, one and one-eighth pound of butter, one-half pound of candied citron, four pounds of currants, four pounds of raisins (stoned and chopped), nine eggs, one table-spoonful each of ground cloves, of cinnamon, of mace, and of nutmeg, and three gills of brandy.

This cake is perhaps not too large, as it will keep for years.

English Pound-cake.

Ingredients: One pound of butter beaten to a cream, one pound of pounded sugar, ten eggs (whites and yolks beaten separately), one pound of dried flour, eight ounces of almonds, eight ounces of candied peel, two wine-glasses of brandy.

When all are well beaten together, add three pounds of English currants and one pound of raisins (both dredged in flour). Set it immediately in a moderate oven, and bake three hours at least.

Boston Cream-cakes.

Paste.—One pint of water, half a pound of butter, three-quarters of a pound of flour, ten eggs.

Boil the water and butter together; stir in the flour while boiling, and let it cook a moment; when cool, add the eggs, well beaten, with a tea-spoonful of saleratus and a little salt. Drop with a spoon on buttered tins, forming little cakes some distance apart. Bake in a quick oven; they will puff in baking. When done and cold, cut one side large enough to insert the cream with a spoon. This will make about sixty cakes.

Cream.—One cupful of flour, two cupfuls of sugar, four eggs, one quart of milk.

Beat the eggs and sugar together, then add flour and enough of the milk to make a smooth and thin paste; pour this into the remainder of the milk when it is boiling, and stir constantly until it is sufficiently thickened; flavor with vanilla. Do not use it until it is cold. It is better to make this, as indeed all custards, in a custard-kettle.

CRULLERS (*Miss Amanda Newton*).

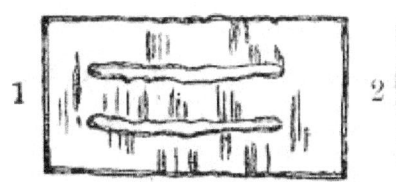  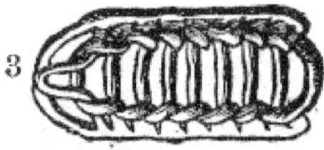

Beat three eggs well with four table-spoonfuls of sugar; add four or five table-spoonfuls of melted lard, then flour enough to make it not too stiff. Roll rather thin (one-third of an inch). Cut the cakes into shapes, and throw them into boiling lard, like doughnuts. They may be simply shaped, as in Fig. 1. To give them the shape of Fig. 3, first cut the paste, as in Fig. 2; hold the first line with the thumb and finger of the left hand, then with the right hand slip the second line under the first, then the third under the second, and so on until they are all slipped under; pinch the two ends together, and the cruller will be in form of Fig. 3.

DOUGHNUTS (*Mrs. Bartlett*).

Ingredients: Two eggs, one cupful of sugar, one cupful of sour milk, half a tea-spoonful of soda, four table-spoonfuls of melted lard; add flour, making the dough rather soft.

Fry them in hot lard, and sprinkle pulverized sugar over them while still hot.

BREAD-CAKE.

Ingredients: Three cupfuls of bread-dough, one cupful of butter, three scant cupfuls of sugar, one cupful of raisins or English currants, three eggs, a nutmeg grated, one tea-spoonful of soda, two of cream of tartar, a wine-glassful of brandy.

GINGERBREAD (*Mrs. Lansing*), No. 1.

Ingredients: Two cupfuls of molasses, one cupful of butter, one cupful of sugar, one cupful of milk (sour or sweet), five eggs, five cupfuls of sifted flour, two table-spoonfuls of ginger, half a tea-spoonful of cloves, one tea-spoonful of soda.

Gingerbread (No. 2).

Ingredients: One cupful (half a pint) of molasses, one cupful (half a pint) of boiling water, butter the size of an egg, one tea-spoonful each of ground cloves, ground cinnamon, ginger, and soda, half a pound of flour (light weight).

First, put butter (partly melted) into the molasses, then spices. Dissolve the soda in the boiling water; stir it into the molasses, etc.; then the flour. Cream of tartar should not be used with molasses.

Chocolate-cake.

Make a cup-cake with the following ingredients: One cupful of butter, two cupfuls of sugar, three cupfuls of flour, one cupful of milk, four eggs beaten separately, one tea-spoonful of soda, two tea-spoonfuls of cream of tartar, or two tea-spoonfuls of yeast powder.

Cut the cup-cake, when baked, through the middle, or bake it in two or three parts. Put a layer of the chocolate mixture between and on the top and sides of the cake.

Chocolate Mixture.—Five table-spoonfuls of grated chocolate, with enough cream or milk to wet it, one cupful of sugar, and one egg well beaten. Stir the ingredients over the fire until thoroughly mixed; then flavor with vanilla.

Mountain-cake.

Ingredients: Whites of six eggs, one and a quarter cupfuls of sugar, one and a quarter cupfuls of flour, half a cupful of butter, half a cupful of sweet milk, half a cupful of corn starch, a little vanilla, two tea-spoonfuls of baking-powder.

Bake it in two or three parts, like jelly-cake; put a frosting between the layers and on top of the cake, made of the whites of four eggs, nine table-spoonfuls of pulverized sugar, and a little vanilla; or use grated cocoa-nut, mixed thickly in the frosting, without vanilla; or use the chocolate mixture in the preceding receipt; or make it a jelly-cake.

Cream Cake or Pie (*Mrs. Arnold*).

This is an excellent dessert cut as a pie, or it may be served as a cake for tea.

Crust.—Three eggs, one cupful of sugar, one cupful of flour, one-third of a tea-spoonful of soda, and one tea-spoonful of cream of tartar. Beat the whites and yolks well separately; stir all together as quickly as possible, and bake in two pans (if rather small; if large, use only one), the batter three-quarters of an inch thick.

Cream.—Two and a half cupfuls of sweet milk, four even table-spoonfuls of sugar, two table-spoonfuls of flour, and one egg. Boil this a few moments until it has thickened, and flavor with vanilla or lemon.

When the crust is cold, split it, and put the custard between.

This cake is much improved with a boiled icing.

Sponge Jelly-cake (*Mrs. Pope*).

Ingredients: Five eggs, one cupful of sugar, one cupful of flour, two even tea-spoonfuls of yeast-powder, and grated rind of a lemon.

Beat the yolks, sugar, and lemon together to a cream; add whites of eggs beaten to a stiff froth; then the flour and yeast-powder perfectly mixed. Bake in a dripping-pan, and when done spread jelly (not sweet) over the bottom of the cake, roll it from the side, and sprinkle sugar over the top; or bake it in two or three jelly-cake pans, and spread jelly between. The cake may be iced on the bottom. The rolled jelly-cake may be cut into slices, and served with a sweet sauce for dessert.

Cocoa-nut Cones.

Ingredients: One pound of cocoa-nut grated, half a pound of sugar, the whites of two eggs, and the yolk of one egg.

Beat the yolk well; add the sugar to it; then the cocoa-nut and whites of the eggs beaten to a stiff froth. Drop by the tea-spoonful on sheets of buttered paper placed on tins. Form each little cake into the shape of a cone, and bake in a moderate oven about half an hour.

Croquante Cake (*Mrs. Lackland*).

Ingredients: Three-quarters of a pound of shelled almonds, half a pound of citron, three-quarters of a pound of sugar, three-quarters of a pound of flour, and six eggs.

Blanch and halve the almonds, and slice the citron; mix them well together, and roll them in flour; add to them the sugar, then the eggs (well beaten), lastly the flour. Butter shallow pans, and lay in the mixture two inches thick. After it is baked in a quick oven, slice the cake into strips one inch wide, and turn every strip. Return the pan to the oven, and bake the sides a little. When cold, put it away in tin boxes. This cake will keep a year or more, and for reserve use is quite invaluable.

To Blanch Almonds.

Put them over the fire in cold water, and let them remain until the water is almost at the boiling-point, not allowing them to boil; then throw them into cold water. Remove the skins, and dry the almonds in a cloth before using.

When they are to be pounded for macaroons, *méringues*, etc., they should be first dried for two or three days in a gentle heat.

Rebecca Cake (*Mrs. North*).

Ingredients: Half a cupful of butter, one cupful of sugar, one cupful of sweet milk, one egg, one pint of flour, one tea-spoonful of soda, and two tea-spoonfuls of cream of tartar.

For a change, a cupful of raisins or of English currants, or a mixture of both, or an addition of sliced citron, may be added.

Ginger-snaps (*Mrs. Leach*).

Ingredients: One pint of molasses, one coffee-cupful of brown sugar, one coffee-cupful of butter, one table-spoonful of ginger, and one heaping tea-spoonful of soda dissolved in one table-spoonful of hot water.

Mix very thick with flour, and roll them very thin.

Plain Cookies.

Ingredients: One cupful of butter (or half butter and half lard), two cupfuls of sugar, one cupful of milk, two eggs, about a quart of flour (cookies are better to have no more flour than is necessary for rolling them thin without sticking), three tea-spoonfuls (not heaping) of yeast-powder, or one tea-spoonful of cream of tartar and half a tea-spoonful of soda.

Sour milk can be used, when add the half tea-spoonful of soda, and omit the cream of tartar. Bake in a quick oven.

Almond Macaroons.

Blanch and skin eight ounces of Jordan almonds and one ounce of bitter ones; dry them on a sieve, and pound them to a smooth paste in a mortar, adding occasionally a very little water, to prevent them from getting oily; add to them five ounces of pulverized sugar, one tea-spoonful of rice flour, and the whites of three eggs beaten to a stiff froth; with a spoon, put this on paper in drops the size of a walnut; bake in a slow oven until they are of a light-brown color, and firmly set; take them from the paper by wetting the under side of it.

Lady's-fingers.

Mix six yolks of eggs with half a pound of powdered sugar; work the preparation with a spoon until it is frothy; then mix into it the whites of six eggs well beaten, and at the same time a quarter of a pound of flour, dried and sifted. Put this batter into a *méringue* bag, and squeeze it through in strips, two or three inches long, and sprinkle over some fine sugar; bake in a slack oven twelve or fourteen minutes.

Méringues à la Crème.

Ingredients: Six whites of eggs, nine ounces of pulverized sugar, half a pint of cream (whipped), three ounces of sugar with the cream, a slight flavoring of vanilla.

Whip the eggs to a very stiff froth, add three or four drops of vanilla, and mix in the pulverized sifted sugar, by turning the sugar all over the eggs at once, and cutting it together very carefully. Sprinkle sugar over a tin platter, and on it place table-spoonfuls of this mixture at convenient distances apart; smooth the tops, and sprinkle a little sugar over them also.

The secret of making *méringues* is in the baking. Put them into a moderate oven, and leave the oven-door open for thirty-five minutes at least. They should not be allowed to color for that time, which would prevent them from drying properly, and a thin paper crust is very undesirable for a *méringue*; in fact, the longer they dry before coloring, the thicker will be the crust. They should be in the oven at least three-quarters of an hour, only allowing them to color slightly the last two or three minutes. While they are still hot, scoop out carefully the soft contents, and when they are cold fill them with whipped cream, press two of them together, forming a ball, and put them into the refrigerator to set the cream.

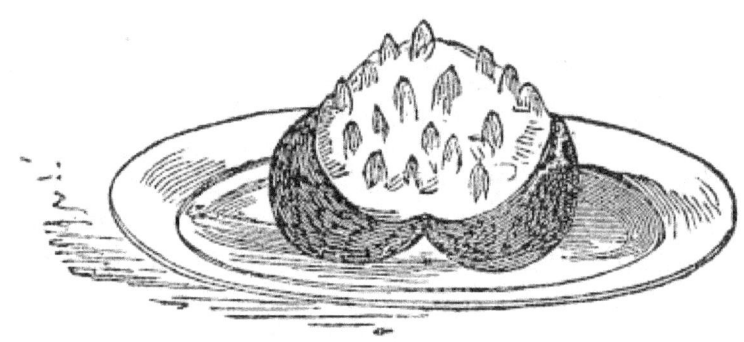

A much prettier arrangement for dessert is the *méringue* as it is fashioned at Delmonico's. Instead of little *méringues*, each one is made a half ball, about six inches in diameter. They are dried very slowly, so that the crust is about one-third of an inch thick. When emptied of the soft interiors, and when cold, two shells are placed on a platter, like an open clam-shell. The whipped cream, when about to serve (already set, by being on the ice), is banked between them, reaching as high above as suits the fancy. The cream may be decorated with strawberries, raspberries, etc., or it may be served without ornamentation.

German Cake (*Mrs. Schulenburg*).

Ingredients: One pound of flour, three-quarters of a pound of butter, six ounces of sugar, one egg, half a cupful of rum.

Bake in a pie-pan, pressing the cake until it is about one-quarter of an inch high. Before baking, sprinkle sugar and ground cinnamon on top; after it is baked, cut it into squares while it is yet warm.

Ranaque Buns.

Ingredients: One pound of butter, one and a quarter pounds of sugar, two pounds of flour, six eggs, four table-spoonfuls of ground cinnamon.

Mix the cinnamon into the flour; rub the butter to a cream, then mix the flour with it. Beat the sugar with the eggs, then all together, as little as possible. Distribute this by the spoonful into rough-looking cakes on buttered tins placed at a little distance apart. This is a very nice lunch-cake.

Frosting.

The old way of making frosting was a half-day's work. I now laugh at the extra exertion once made to be sure that the eggs were sufficiently and properly beaten. The following is the true way to make frosting, which is done and dried on the cake in ten minutes, allowing three minutes for the making:

Use a heaping tea-cupful of fine pulverized sugar to the white of each egg, or, say, a pound of sugar to the whites of three eggs. Beat the whites until they are slightly *foaming* only; do not beat them to a froth. The sugar may all be poured on the egg at once, or, if considered easier to mix, it may be gradually added. Either way, as soon as the sugar and eggs are thoroughly stirred together, and flavored with a little lemon or vanilla, the icing is ready to spread over the cake. It would be advisable to ice the cakes as soon as they are taken from the oven. The icing made with the white of one egg is quite sufficient to frost an ordinary-sized cake.

It is very little extra trouble to decorate a frosted cake. One can purchase funnels for the purpose with different shaped ends. In place of no better funnel, make a cornucopia of stiff writing-paper; fill it with the frosting, and press it out at the small end, forming different shapes, according to taste, over the cake. Little centre-pieces or leaves can always be purchased at the confectioner's to aid in the decoration.

For a cocoa-nut-cake, mix plenty of the grated cocoa-nut into the frosting, which spread over the cake; decorate it then with plain frosting.

For a chocolate-cake, after spreading over the chocolate frosting mentioned in the receipt for chocolate-cake, decorate it with delicate lines of the white frosting.

The appearance of boiled icing (which is generally flavored with lemon) is much improved also by a decoration with the plain white frosting.

Boiled Icing.

Ingredients: One pound of sugar, whites of three eggs.

First, boil the sugar with a little water; when it is ready to candy, or will spin in threads when dropping from the end of a spoon, take it off the fire, and while it is still boiling hot add the whites of the eggs *well* beaten, stirring them in as fast as possible. Flavor with lemon (if preferred), vanilla, Jamaica rum, or any of the flavorings, and it is ready for use.

CANDIES.

Caramels (*Mrs. Wadsworth*).

Ingredients: One cupful of best sirup, one cupful of brown sugar, one cupful of white sugar, two cupfuls of grated chocolate, two cupfuls of cream, vanilla, one tea-spoonful of flour mixed with the cream.

Rub the chocolate to a smooth paste with a little of the cream; boil all together half an hour, and pour it into flat dishes to cool; mark it with a knife into little squares when it is cool enough.

White-sugar Candy (*Miss Eliza Brown*).

Ingredients: Four pounds of sugar, one pint of water, four table-spoonfuls of cream, four table-spoonfuls of vinegar, butter the size of an egg.

Boil all together slowly for about three-quarters of an hour.

Vinegar Candy (*Mrs. Clifford*).

Ingredients: Three cupfuls of sugar, half a cupful of vinegar, half a cupful of water, one tea-spoonful of soda.

When it boils, stir in the soda. If the candy is preferred clear, stir it as little as possible; if grained, stir it.

ICES.

With a patent five-minute freezer (it really takes, however, from fifteen minutes to half an hour to freeze any thing), it is as cheap and easy to make ices in summer as almost any other kind of dessert. If one has cream, the expense is very little, as a cream-whipper costs but twenty-five cents. A simple cream, sweetened, flavored, whipped, and then frozen, is one of the most delicious of ice-creams. By having the cream quite cold, a pint can be whipped, with this cream-whipper, in five or ten minutes. It will require ten cents' worth of ice—half of it to freeze the preparation, and the other half to keep it frozen until the time of serving. Salt is not proverbially expensive; a half-barrel or bushel of coarse salt will last a long time, especially as a portion of it can be used a second time. In summer, fruits, such as peaches or pears, quartered, or any kind of berries, are most delicious half frozen and served with sugar. The chocolate ice-cream with fruit is excellent. The devices of form for creams served at handsome dinners in large cities are very beautiful; for instance, one sees a hen surrounded by her chickens; or a hen sitting on the side of a spun-glass nest, looking sideways at her eggs; or a fine collection of fruits in colors. One may see also a perfect imitation of asparagus with a cream-dressing, the asparagus being made of the *pistache* cream, and the dressing simply a whipped cream. These fancy displays are, of course, generally arranged by the confectioner. It is a convenience, of course, when giving dinner companies, to have the dessert or any other course made outside of the house; but for ordinary occasions, ices are no more troublesome to prepare than any thing else, especially when they can be made early in the day, or even the day before serving.

Frozen Whipped Cream.

Flavor and sweeten the cream, making it rather sweet. Whip it, and freeze the froth.

Vanilla Ice-cream.

Beat the yolks of eight eggs with three-quarters of a pound of sugar until very light. Put one and a half pints of rich milk on the fire to scald, highly flavored with the powdered vanilla-bean (say, one heaping table-spoonful). When the milk is well scalded, stir it into the eggs as soon as it is cool enough not to curdle. Now stir the mixture constantly (the custard pan or pail being set in a vessel of boiling water) until it has slightly thickened. Do not let it remain too long and curdle, or it will be spoiled. When taken off the fire again, mix in a quarter of a box of gelatine, which has been soaked half an hour in two table-spoonfuls of lukewarm water near the fire. The heat of the custard will be sufficient to dissolve it, if it is not already sufficiently dissolved. Cool the custard well before putting it into the freezer, as this saves time and ice. When it is in the freezer, however, stir it almost constantly until it begins to set; then stir in lightly a pint of cream, whipped. Stir it for two or three minutes longer, put it into a mold, and return it to a second relay of ice and salt. The powdered vanilla can be purchased at drug-stores or at confectioners'. It is much better than the extract for any purpose, and is used by all the best *restaurateurs*.

Delmonico Vanilla Cream.

Ingredients: One and a half pints of cream, one ounce of isinglass, one pound of sugar, yolks of eight eggs, half a pint of milk, vanilla powder.

Scald the cream only; then add the isinglass dissolved in the milk, and pour it on the sugar and eggs beaten together to a froth; add the flavoring. Strain, cool, and freeze it; then pack it for three hours and a half at least.

Chocolate Ice-cream

is made in the same way as the vanilla ice-cream, adding a flavoring of chocolate and a little vanilla powder. For instance, to make a quart and a half of cream: Make the boiled custard with the yolks of six eggs, half a pound of sugar, one pint of boiled milk, and a tea-spoonful (not heaping) of vanilla powder. Pound smooth four ounces of chocolate; add a little sugar and one or two table-spoonfuls of hot water. Stir it over the fire until it is perfectly smooth. Add this and a table-spoonful of thin, dissolved gelatine to the hot custard. When about to set in the freezer, add one pint of cream, whipped.

To Make a Mold of Chocolate and Vanilla Creams.

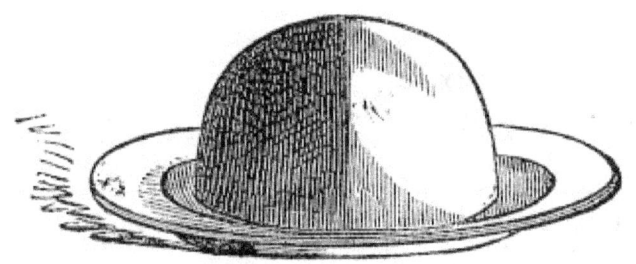

Freeze the different creams in two freezers. Cut a piece of pasteboard to fit the centre of a mold; fill each side with the two creams, remove the pasteboard, and imbed the mold in ice and salt for two hours.

Strawberry Ice-cream.

Sprinkle sugar over strawberries, mash them well, and rub them through a sieve. To a pint of the juice add half a pint of good cream. Make it very sweet. Freeze it in the usual way, and, when beginning to set, stir in lightly one pint of cream (whipped), and, lastly, a handful of whole strawberries, sweetened. Put it into a mold, which imbed in ice. Or, when fresh strawberries can not be obtained, there is no more delicious cream than that made with the French bottled strawberries. Mix the juice in the bottle with the cream, and add the whipped cream and the whole strawberries, when the juice, etc., have partly set in the freezer.

Many prefer this cream of a darker red color, which is obtained by using prepared cochineal.

Napolitaine Cream.

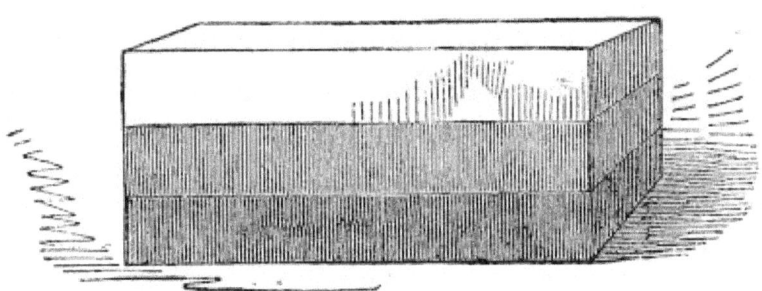

To make a form of three colors: Vanilla, chocolate, and strawberry ice-creams are frozen in three different freezers, and filled in a mold the form of a brick in three smooth layers of equal size.

Chocolate Fruit Ice-cream.

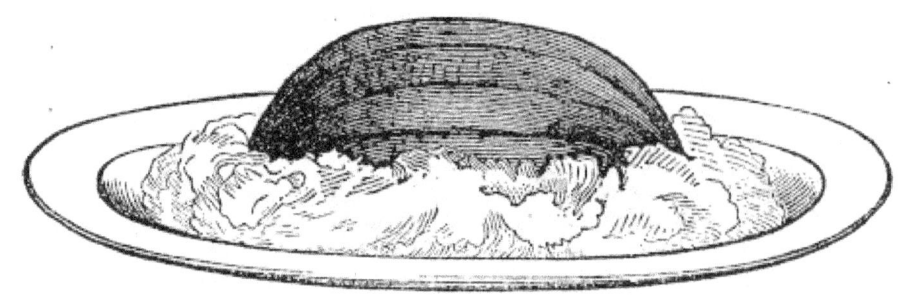

Make a chocolate cream. When set in the freezer, add about half a pound of assorted French candied or preserved fruits cut into small pieces. Put it into a melon-shaped mold, to imitate a plum-pudding. When ready to serve, turn the cream on a platter, and make a circle around it of whipped cream, sweetened and flavored with vanilla. This cream is a decided success, and a beautiful dessert for a dinner-party. It may be improved by sprinkling over it chopped almonds dried of a light-brown color, mixed with chopped pistachios. This is intended to imitate the rugged appearance of the rind of a melon.

Frozen Fruit Custard.

Ingredients: One pint of rich milk, one pint of cream (whipped), yolks of three eggs, one and a half cupfuls of sugar, one pint of fresh peaches cut into pieces not too small, or fresh ripe berries.

Beat the eggs and sugar well together. Heat the pint of milk almost to the boiling-point, and add it gradually to the beaten eggs and sugar. Return it to the custard-kettle, and stir it constantly until it has slightly thickened, taking care that it does not curdle. When the custard is partly frozen, having stirred it in the usual way, add the whipped cream; stir a few minutes longer, and then stir in the fruit. Put all into a mold, which place in a fresh relay of ice and salt.

German Steamer Baked Ice-cream.

This dish was at least a curiosity, served at the table of one of the German steamers. A flat, round sponge-cake served as a base. A circular mold of very hard frozen ice-cream was placed on this, and then covered with a *méringue*, or whipped white of egg, sweetened and flavored. The surface was quickly colored with a red-hot salamander, which gave the dish the appearance of being baked.

The gentleman who told me about this dish insisted that it was put into the oven and quickly colored, as the egg surrounding the cream was a sufficiently good non-conductor of heat to protect the ice for one or two minutes. However, there is less risk with a salamander.

PINE-APPLE ICE-CREAM PUDDING.

Add one pound of pine-apple grated fine to the yolks of eight eggs well beaten with one pound of sugar, one and a half pints of boiled cream, and a very little salt. Stir all together over the fire until it begins to thicken. When beginning to set in the freezer (having stirred it in the usual way), add a pint of cream (whipped). This addition of the whipped cream is a great improvement, although it is generally omitted. Put it into a form. When ready to serve, press the tuft of leaves, cut from the pine-apple and trimmed, in the top of the cream. Surround it with whipped and sweetened cream.

ICED RICE-PUDDING (*Francatelli*).

Wash and parboil half a pound of rice; then put it into a stew-pan, with a quart of milk and a pint of cream, two sticks of vanilla, three-quarters of a pound of sugar, and a little salt. Allow the rice to simmer very gently over or by a slow fire, until the grains are almost dissolved, stirring it occasionally with a light hand. When the rice is done, and while it is yet hot, add the yolks of six eggs; then stir all well together for several minutes, in order to mix in the eggs, and also for the purpose of breaking up and smoothing the rice. Let this rice custard be frozen like an ordinary ice-cream, stirring it from the sides until it is set, when put it into a mold, and immerse it in the ice and salt.

While the above part of the process is going on, a *compôte* of twelve oranges should be prepared in the following manner: First, separate them into sections, and remove every particle of the white pith with a small knife, laying the transparent pulp of the fruit quite bare. When all the oranges are ready, throw them into a stew-pan containing about a pint of sirup (made with one pound of sugar and nearly a pint of clear water); allow the pieces of oranges to boil up gently in this for two minutes, and then drain them in a sieve. Boil the sirup down to about one-half of its original quantity; then add two wine-glassfuls of curaçoa and three table-spoonfuls of peach marmalade or apricot jam; mix all together, and pour this preparation over the oranges in a basin. When about to send the pudding to table, turn it out of the mold on a platter, dress the *compôte* of oranges on the top and around the base, pour the sirup over it, and serve.

Biscuit Glacés, in Small Cases.

Beat well eight yolks of eggs, with ten ounces of sugar, and a very little salt; add one pint of cream. Stir over the fire until slightly thickened. Flavor with vanilla powder, the extract of almonds, lemon, or with coffee or chocolate. It may also be made by adding a *purée* of peaches, strawberries, raspberries, or pine-apple to the custard. When just beginning to set in the freezer, stir in lightly one-half pint of cream (whipped); then partly fill paper cases with the mixture. Smooth over the tops. Set the cases in the freezer well dried, and allow them to harden until ready to serve.

Biscuit Glacés (*Francatelli*).

Ingredients: One pint of clarified sirup, twelve yolks of eggs, two whole eggs, a large wine-glassful of maraschino.

Mix the whole of the ingredients in an earthen basin; then pour the preparation into an egg-bowl that has been previously warmed with hot water and wiped dry. Whisk the *soufflé* briskly (the egg bowl being placed on a stove containing hot ashes) until it resembles a well-prepared, firm, sponge-cake batter. Fill the paper cases with the preparation, and smooth over the tops. Place them in a tin pail or in the freezer, surrounded with ice and salt, and half a pound of saltpetre mixed, and let them remain well covered for three or four hours at least, before serving, without stirring them. Or, they may be frozen all together in one mold, and some sifted macaroon powder or grated chocolate sprinkled over the surface, to imitate a baked *soufflé*.

Nesselrode Pudding (*Carême's Receipt*).

Ingredients: Forty chestnuts, one pound of sugar, flavoring of vanilla, one pint of cream, the yolks of twelve eggs, one glass of maraschino, one ounce of candied citron, two ounces of currants, two ounces of stoned raisins.

Blanch the chestnuts in boiling water, remove the husks, and pound them in a mortar until perfectly smooth, adding a few spoonfuls of the sirup; then rub them through a fine sieve, and mix them in a basin with a pint of sirup, made from one pound of sugar, clarified, and flavored with vanilla; one pint of cream, and the yolks of twelve eggs. Set this mixture over a slow fire, stirring it *without ceasing*, until the eggs begin to thicken (without allowing them to curdle), then take it off. When it is cold, put it into the freezer, adding the maraschino, and make the mixture set; then add the sliced citron, the currants, and stoned raisins (these two latter should be soaked the day previous in maraschino, and sugar pounded with vanilla) to the whole. Thus mingled, add a plateful of whipped cream, mixed with the whites of three eggs beaten to a froth. When the pudding is perfectly frozen, put it into a mold, close the lid, place it again in the freezer, well surrounded with pounded ice and saltpetre, and let it remain until the time of serving, when turn it out of the mold.

Iced Pudding.

Ingredients: One and one-half pints of custard, composed of the yolks of four eggs, a pint of boiled milk, four table-spoonfuls of sugar, a flavoring of vanilla, eight ounces of fruits, consisting of equal parts of dried cherries, pine-apple, dried pears, or apricots, all cut into very small squares. These fruits may be selected, or perhaps it would be more convenient to purchase half a pound of the French preserved dried fruits; or add one ounce of candied citron sliced, two ounces of currants, two ounces of stoned and chopped raisins, and half a pint of cream whipped.

Freeze the custard in the usual manner, then mix in the fruits and whipped cream. A gill of maraschino is an improvement to this pudding, but may be omitted. If added, it should be at the same time with the fruit. Put into a mold, and place it on ice and salt. Serve whipped cream around it.

Tutti Frutti.

When a rich vanilla cream is partly frozen, candied cherries, English currants, chopped raisins, chopped citron, or any other candied fruits chopped rather fine, are added; add about the same quantity of fruit as there is of ice cream. Mold and imbed in ice and salt. It may be served surrounded with a whipped cream.

Fresh Peaches Half Frozen.

An exceedingly nice dish for breakfast, lunch, or tea may be made of quarters of large fresh peaches, *half* frozen, and then sprinkled with granulated sugar.

Peaches and Cream Frozen.

Peel and quarter the fresh peaches; mix them with sugar and cream to taste. Arrange some of the quarters of the peaches tastefully in the bottom of a basin, or *charlotte* mold, then fill, and freeze the mass solid, without stirring. Turn it out to serve.

Lemon Ice.

Boil three pints of water and one quart of loaf-sugar until reduced to nearly one quart of liquid, skimming it when necessary. When cold, add the juice of seven lemons, and the thin-sliced yellow part of the rind of four of them. Let it infuse an hour. Strain it into the freezer without pressing. When beginning to set in the freezer, stir in lightly and well the beaten whites of four eggs. Put into a mold, and return it to a fresh relay of salt and ice. Or it may be frozen and served in the lemon-skins. A neat slice is taken off the top of the lemon. The juice, etc., is carefully removed. When the preparation is set in the freezer, the skins are filled, the tops fitted over, and all imbedded in the ice. I once saw at one of Delmonico's dinners a course of these lemons (one for each person) filled with Roman punch.

Currant Ice.

Boil one quart of water and a pound of sugar until reduced about a pint —*i. e.*, until a pint of water has boiled away; skim it, take it off the fire, and add a pint of currant-juice; when partly frozen, stir in the beaten whites of four eggs. Mold, and freeze again. A good ice for fever patients.

COOKERY FOR THE SICK.

I believe it is the general practice now to give a patient, in almost every kind of illness, food that is very nourishing, yet very digestible, that the system may become strengthened to throw off its disease.

I devote a chapter to "cookery for the sick," as it is such a useful and delightful accomplishment to know just how to prepare the few available dishes for invalids, so that while they may be most suitable food for the recovery of the patient, they may at the same time be most agreeable to the taste and pleasing to the eye.

The three events of the day to the sufferer are the three meals. How gratefully is it remembered if they have been delicately and carefully administered! Let the mother or the wife prepare them with her own hands; let her never ask an invalid what he will have to eat, but with thought and ingenuity strive to vary the bill of fare each day, always providing proper nourishment. This is an art in itself which can be delegated to no one. It is worth as much to the suffering and beloved patient as is the medical prescription of the physician.

Never leave an article of diet in the sick-room: it is a good means of destroying the appetite, which should be encouraged and not weakened.

Whatever is served, let great attention be paid to giving the dish, after it is properly cooked, a dainty appearance. Place it on the choicest of ware in the house, with the cleanest of napkins, and the brightest of silver, even if that consists only of a tea-spoon.

If tea and toast be served, put the tea, freshly drawn, into the daintiest of tea-cups. Every family might well afford to buy one little, thin china cup and saucer, to use in case of illness; put a square of loaf-sugar into it. A few drops of cream are easily saved for the patient's tea from a small quantity of milk; and cream in small quantities is considered more digestible than milk.

All cooks think they can make toast. There is about one person in ten thousand who really does know how to make it; who actually appreciates the difference between a thin, symmetrical, well-yellowed, crisp piece of toast with the crust cut off, and just from the fire, and a thick, unshapely slice, unevenly crisped on the outside, and of doughy softness in the centre.

One is digestible; the other is exceedingly indigestible. The *scientific* mode of making toast is explained on page 67.

Of the laxative articles of diet, undoubtedly one of the most important is the oatmeal porridge. The chemists say, "Oatmeal stands before all other grains in point of nutritive power." I do not mean to serve gruel, but a thicker preparation, of considerable consistence, which is more palatable. The mode of making it is explained on page 74. Put a heaping tablespoonful of this on a thin saucer; pour some cream over it; then sprinkle over this a little granulated sugar. Now place the saucer on a little salver, on which is spread the whitest of napkins.

Always remember that in cooking any of the grains, as, for instance, corn-meal, oatmeal, hominy, cracked-wheat, etc., let them be thrown into *salted boiling* water. This makes very great difference in the flavor of the dish. Make every thing in small quantities, so that the patient may always have his dishes *freshly* made.

A very nourishing, digestible, and excellent dish for invalids is a raw, fresh egg, the receipt for administering which is given among the invalid receipts

In regard to rice, Dr. Lee remarks: "We regard rice as the most valuable of all the articles of food in cases of the derangement of the digestive organs. It nourishes, while it soothes the irritable mucous membrane; and while it supports strength, never seems to aggravate the existing disease. For acute or chronic affections of the alimentary canal, rice-water for drink and rice-jelly for food seem peculiarly well adapted, and appear to exert a specific influence in bringing about a recovery. These preparations are invaluable also in convalescence from acute fevers and other maladies, and in the summer complaints of young children."

Jellies made with gelatine or calf's feet are very appetizing, but must not be relied on as furnishing much nourishment. They afford a pleasant vehicle for administering wine, of which the stimulating properties are often very advantageous. I copy a short article from Booth's "Chemistry" on the subject:

"Gelatine in domestic economy is used in the forms of soup and jelly as an aliment; but though experiments seem to show that when mixed with fibrous, albuminous, and caseous substances it becomes nutritive, this conclusion is yet doubtful; for the theory of respiration proves that histrose, which produces the gelatine, has accomplished its part in the animal organization, and can no longer afford sustenance thereto. One fact, however, seems positive, and that is its inability alone to yield nourishment to carnivorous animals. The feeble nutritive power of a gelatinous matter seems to be owing to the destruction of its organization."

On the same subject of the dietetical value of gelatine, Professor Youmans says: "It is regarded as a product of the partial decomposition of albuminous bodies in the system, but as incapable of replacing them when taken as aliment. The French attempted to feed the inmates of their hospitals on gelatinous extract of bones. Murmurs arose, and a commission, with Magendie at their head, was appointed to investigate the matter. They reported gelatine as, dietetically, almost worthless."

Graham bread, corn bread, or the Boston brown-bread, made with part rye flour, are much more nourishing than breads made from bolted wheat. The whiter the wheat flour, the more starch it contains, and the less gluten, which is separated in bolting, and which is the nutritious or flesh-producing portion. The rich Boston brown-bread is especially good cut into thin, even pieces, with a little cream poured over it.

The value of corn-meal for invalids who are thin and incapable of maintaining their natural warmth is scarcely appreciated. Indian-corn contains a large percentage of oil, which is nourishing and fattening. Fat is the heat-producing power.

As to the meats, it seems to me a mistake that that from the ox, with his wholesome food, cleanly habits, sweet breath, and clear eye, is not the most wholesome and digestible of aliments. No meat is so tender and juicy as the cut from the tenderloin or the porter-house steak.

Pork should be avoided in every form by invalids.

I can not but believe that rare-cooked, tender beef is the most valuable dish in the culinary *répertoire* for invalids; yet Dr. Beaumont, after experimenting with St. Martin, ranks venison, when tender and in season, as the most digestible and assimilable of meats. He classes mutton second; then beef. Lamb is less digestible than mutton. Veal should be avoided as well as pork. Fatty substances are also difficult of assimilation. Poultry is less digestible than beef. Then, again, the manner of cooking beef has a great influence on its digestibility. The best modes are broiling and roasting. Potatoes roasted or baked are digested an hour sooner than potatoes boiled.

Before beginning the receipts for especial dishes, I will copy a little story, which furnishes an illustration that the simplest modes of cooking are, after all, the most satisfactory.

"The Vicomte de Vaudreuil, when appointed *chargé d'affaires* of France to the Court of St. James's, brought over with him a young cook, an *élève* of the highest schools of the *cuisines* of Paris. This young culinary aspirant to fame, shortly after his arrival in London, obtained permission of his master to go and witness the artistic operations of that established *cordon-bleu*, Monsieur Mingay, the cook to Prince Esterhazy, who had been brought up under the Prince Talleyrand's famous *chef*, Louis, and previously under that most *bleu* of all *cordons*, the great Carême. On the *élève's* return, the Vicomte, hearing that his cook was in a state of astonishment from something he had witnessed in Prince Esterhazy's kitchen, summoned him to his presence, and said, 'What is this culinary miracle, which I have heard astonishes you, and casts into the shade all other triumphs of the art?' Vatel's follower replied, 'Oh, Monsieur le Vicomte, when I entered the *cuisine* at Chandos House it was near the time of the prince's luncheon, for which his excellency had ordered something which should be very simple and easily digestible, as he was suffering from languor. The *chef*, Mingay, accordingly cut from under a well-hung rump of beef three slices of fillet, and rapidly broiling them, he placed the choicest-looking in the middle of a hot dish, and afterward pressing the juice completely out of the remaining two, he poured it on the first! Oh, monsieur, how great the prince! how great the cook!'"

RECEIPTS FOR THE SICK-ROOM.

Tea.

Tea is best, made fresh in the sick-room. A little *tête-à-tête* china service is a pretty ornament for a bedroom, and it is a convenient and tasteful arrangement for serving tea to invalids. If one has no little tea-pot like that belonging to the service here referred to, a small one of any other kind is desirable.

Put two tea-spoonfuls of tea-leaves into the small tea-pot; pour two tea-cupfuls of *boiling* water over it; cover it closely, and let it steam for a few moments.

With a small table at the side of the invalid's bed, it is a decidedly pleasant little diversion to make tea in this manner, being sure at the same time that it is perfectly fresh. However it is made though, do not present a cupful of tea to a sufferer with a part of the tea spilled into the saucer.

To avoid having fat left in the soups, it is safer to allow them to get entirely cold, when the fat can be easily skimmed off. Just enough can be heated each time the soup is served.

Beef Tea, or Essence of Beef.

Cut, say, a pound of perfectly lean beef into small pieces, put them into a wide-mouthed bottle (a pickle-bottle answers the purpose), cork it tightly, and place it in a pot of *cold* water in which there is a saucer at the bottom. Heat it gradually, then let it boil slowly for two or three hours, when all the juice will be drawn out of the meat.

Now pour off the juice, season it with salt carefully, as it requires very little. When it is cold, skim off all the globules of fat.

This is an invaluable aliment for invalids who are very ill, or for weak infants, when they need much nourishment in small compass. This beef tea can then be given by the tea-spoonful at regular intervals, administering it as medicine.

Another Beef Tea (*for Convalescents*).

Soak three-quarters of a pound of small-cut pieces of lean steak (say a cut from a round steak) in a pint of cold rain-water for half an hour, squeezing the beef occasionally; then put it on the fire, cover it, and boil it slowly for ten minutes, removing the scum. Season with salt, and serve hot. Serve Albert biscuit, or thin wafers (see page 72), with it. The addition of a little boiled rice makes a pleasant change.

Beef Juice.

Choose a thick cut of fine, fresh, juicy steak without fat. Broil it over the coals for only a minute, or long enough to merely heat it throughout. Put it over a warm bowl set in a basin of hot water; cut it in many places, and squeeze out all the juice with the aid of the meat-squeezer (see page 56). Salt it very slightly. It should be served immediately, freed from every atom of fat, and accompanied with a wafer cracker.

Chicken Broth.

Cut up a fowl, and crack the bones. Put it into three pints of cold water. Boil it slowly, closely covered, for three or four hours, or until the meat falls in pieces. Strain it, then add two table-spoonfuls of rice which has been soaked for half an hour in a very little warm water, also a chopped sprig of parsley, if you have it. Simmer it for twenty minutes longer, or until the rice is thoroughly cooked. Season with salt and pepper, but not too highly. Serve with crackers, which should be broken into the broth the last minute.

Chicken Custard.

Ingredients: One half-pint of chicken broth, beaten yolks of three eggs, a little salt. Mix well, and cook it in the custard-kettle (as for boiled custard) until it has thickened. Serve in custard-cups.

Chicken Panada.

Roast a small chicken, and take out the breasts, or use more of the meat if preferred, and add a little salt; chop it as fine as possible, pound it, and pass it through a colander. Soak half the amount of the crumb of French rolls, or good bread (not too fresh), in tepid milk; squeeze it nearly dry, and mix it with the chicken. Thin it with a little strong chicken broth (which may be made with the remainder of the chicken) or with boiling water. Serve it in a custard-cup, to be eaten with a spoon. For convalescents, a very little finely minced parsley may be added.

Mold of Chicken Jelly.

Cut half a raw chicken into small pieces, and break the bones; put it on the fire with a quart of cold water. Boil it slowly until it is reduced to less than half; season with salt and a little pepper, if the invalid is not too ill for pepper. Strain it first through a colander, then a jelly-bag, into a mold or a bowl. If the chicken is quite tender, broil carefully the breast of the other half of it; cut it into dice, or put it whole into the mold or bowl, and cover it with the liquid. When the jelly has hardened, scrape off the layer of fat at the top of the mold before turning the jelly on a little oval platter.

Chicken and Ceylon Moss.

Cut a small fowl (two pounds) into small pieces, and put it over the fire with three pints of cold water, four ounces of Ceylon moss (which can be obtained at the drug-stores), and half a tea-spoonful of salt. Boil all together an hour; then strain it through a jelly-strainer or napkin into little cups or molds.

Mutton Broth

may be made in the same manner as chicken broth, allowing a quart of cold water to each pound of meat.

Veal and Sago Broth (*Marian Harland*).

Ingredients: Two pounds of knuckle of veal cracked to pieces, two quarts of cold water, three table-spoonfuls of best pearl sago soaked in a cupful of cold water, one cupful of cream heated to boiling, and the yolks of two eggs beaten light.

Boil the veal and water in a covered saucepan very slowly until reduced to one quart of liquid; strain, season with salt, and stir in the soaked sago (having previously warmed it by setting for half an hour in a saucepan of boiling water, and stirring from time to time). Simmer half an hour, taking care it does not burn; beat in the cream and eggs. Give one good boil up, and turn out.

Beef and Tapioca Broth.

Soak one pound of beef, cut into pieces, in a quart of cold water for half an hour; then boil it slowly, keeping it closely covered for two hours. Strain it. The last half hour, add half a cupful of tapioca (which has been soaked an hour in a little water), a small sprig of parsley, and a thin cut from an onion. When done, remove the parsley and onion; season with a very little pepper and salt, and two or three drops only of lemon-juice. When just ready to serve, put into the soup an egg, carefully poached in salted water, the white being merely set.

If patients are not too ill, any kind of beef soup made from stock, as explained on page 80, ought to be advantageous.

How To Prepare an Uncooked Egg.

This is a delicate, strengthening, and valuable preparation for an invalid.

Beat well the yolk and a tea-spoonful of sugar in a goblet; then stir in one or two tea-spoonfuls of brandy, sherry, or port wine. Add to this mixture the white of the egg beaten to a stiff froth. Stir all well together. It should quite fill the goblet. If wine is not desired, flavor the egg with nutmeg. It is very palatable without any flavoring at all.

Tapioca Jelly.

Ingredients: One cupful of tapioca, four cupfuls of water, juice and a little of the grated rind of one lemon, and sugar to taste.

Soak the tapioca for four or five hours in the water. Sweeten it, and set it in a pan of boiling water to cook an hour, or until it is thoroughly done and quite clear, stirring it frequently. When nearly cooked, stir in the lemon; and when done, pour it into little molds. Serve with cream sweetened and flavored.

Sea-moss Blanc-mange.

Wash the moss well, and soak it for half an hour or more in a little cold water. To half an ounce or a handful of moss allow one quart of water, or rather of rich milk, if the patient can take milk. When the water or milk is boiling, add the soaked sea-moss, and sugar to taste. Let them simmer until the moss is entirely dissolved. Strain the juice into cups or little molds. Many boil a stick of cinnamon with the water or milk, and flavor also with wine; but the simple flavor of the sea-moss is very pleasant. It may be served with a little cream and sugar poured over it.

Arrowroot Jelly or Blanc-mange.

Add two heaping tea-spoonfuls of best arrowroot, rubbed smooth with a little cold water, to a coffee-cupful of *boiling* water or rich milk which has been sweetened with two tea-spoonfuls of sugar. Stir and boil it until it has thickened. It may be flavored with lemon-juice if made with water, or with brandy or wine if made with milk. It is very nice without flavoring. Pour into a cup or little mold. Serve with cream and sugar poured over, or with a *compote* of fruit around it.

Corn-starch and Rice Puddings

are explained among the regular receipts for puddings. Little circular molds come in form of Fig. A, on page 59. It is a pretty form for any of these puddings or blanc-manges, with a *compote* of apples, peaches, plums, or any other kind of fruit, in the centre.

Rice Jelly.

Mix enough water to two heaping tea-spoonfuls of rice flour to make a thin paste; then add to it a coffee-cupful of boiling-water. Sweeten to taste with loaf-sugar. Boil it until it is transparent. Flavor by boiling with it a stick of cinnamon if the jelly is intended for a patient with summer complaint; or add, instead, several drops of lemon-juice if intended for a patient with fever. Mold it.

Vanilla should never be used for flavoring any dish for an invalid. Homeopathic books can never say enough about its poisonous effects on even healthy and *robust* persons.

Rice-water for Drink

is made in the same way, in the proportion of a table-spoonful of rice flour to a quart of boiling water.

Jelly and Ice (*for Fever Patients*).

Break ice into small pieces about as large as a pea; mix with it about the same quantity of lemon jelly, also cut into little pieces. This is very refreshing.

Parched Rice.

Parch rice to a nice brown, as you would coffee. Throw it into a little *boiling* salted water, and boil it until it is thoroughly done. Do not stir it more than necessary, on account of breaking the grains. Serve with cream and sugar.

Milk Porridge.

Put a dozen raisins into two cupfuls of milk. Bring it to a boil; then add a *heaping* tea-spoonful of flour rubbed to a paste with a little cold water or milk; boil it three or four minutes. The raisins may not be eaten, yet they give a pleasant flavor to the milk; in fact, they may be taken out if the dish is intended for a child.

For a change, the well-beaten white of an egg may be stirred into this preparation *just after* it is taken from the fire, and, again, the raisins may be left out, and the porridge simply flavored with salt or sugar, or sugar and nutmeg.

Beef Sandwich.

Scrape very fine two or three table-spoonfuls of fresh, juicy, *tender*, uncooked beef; season it slightly with pepper and salt; spread it between two thin slices of slightly buttered bread; cut it neatly into little diamonds about two and a half inches long and an inch wide.

Prepared Flour for Summer Complaints (*Mrs. Horace Mann*).

Tie up a pint of flour very tightly in a cloth, and put it into boiling water, and let it boil three hours. When untied, the gluten of the flour will be found in a mass on the outside of the ball. Remove this, and the inside will prove a dry powder which is very astringent. Grate this, and wet a portion of it in cold milk. Boil a pint of milk, and when it is at the boiling-point stir in as much of the wet mixture as will thicken it to the quality of palatable porridge. Stir in a little salt, and let this be the article of diet until the disease is removed. Relieve it at first by toasted bread, or a mutton broth, which latter is also astringent. If the disease has not progressed to the degree of inflammation, this diet will generally preclude all need of medicine.

The author would also add, for a change of diet, well-boiled rice with a little cream, parched rice, beef juice, toasted water or milk crackers, a little tea (avoiding generally too much liquid), and a little wild-cherry brandy; or to Mrs. Mann's flour porridge, when cooked, and just taken hot from the fire, the well-beaten white of an egg might be added; and, after stirring them well together, the preparation should be served immediately.

Milk Toast.

Toast one or two thin slices of bread with the crust cut off; if there are two slices, have them of equal size. When still hot, spread evenly over them a very little fresh butter, and sprinkle over some salt. Now pour over a small tea-cupful of boiling milk, thickened with half a tea-spoonful of flour, and salted to taste. If the invalid can not take milk, the toast may be moistened with boiling water. Serve immediately. It is a very appetizing dish, when fresh made and hot.

Panada.

Sprinkle a little salt or sugar between two large Boston, soda, or Graham crackers, or hard pilot-biscuit; put them into a bowl; pour over just enough boiling water to soak them well; put the bowl into a vessel of boiling water, and let it remain fifteen or twenty minutes, until the crackers are quite clear and like a jelly, but not broken. Then lift them carefully, without breaking, into a hot saucer. Sprinkle on more sugar or salt if desired: a few spoonfuls of sweet, thick cream poured over are a good addition for a change. Never make more than enough for the patient at one time, as they are very palatable when freshly made, and quite insipid if served cold.

Toasted bread cut into thin even slices may be served in the same way. This is also a good baby diet.

A panada may be made by adding an ounce of grated bread or rolled crackers to half a pint of boiling water, slightly salted, and allowing it to boil three or four minutes. It may be sweetened, and flavored with wine or nutmeg, or both; or the sugar and nutmeg may be simply sprinkled over.

Ash-cake.

Wet corn-meal, salted to taste, with enough cold water to make a soft dough, and let it stand half an hour or longer; mold it into an oblong cake, about an inch and a half or two inches thick. A clean spot should then be swept on the hot hearth, the bread placed on it, and covered with hot wood-ashes. The bread is thus steamed before it is baked. It should be done in a half to three-quarters of an hour, and brushed and wiped before eaten. There is no better food than this for dyspeptics inclined to acidity of the stomach, on account of the alkaline properties of the ashes left in the crust. In other extreme cases of dyspepsia where acids are required, I have heard of cures being effected by the use of buttermilk.

Milk Punch.

Sweeten a glass of milk to taste, and add one or two table-spoonfuls of best brandy. Grate a little nutmeg over the top.

Egg-and-milk Punch.

Stir well a heaping tea-spoonful of sugar, and the yolk of an egg together in a goblet, then add a table-spoonful of best brandy. Fill the glass with milk until it is three-quarters full, then stir well into the mixture the white of the egg beaten to a stiff froth. The receipt for "Eggnog" among the "Beverages" is similar to this, and better, of course, as whipped cream is substituted for milk.

Herb Teas

are made by pouring boiling water over one or two tea-spoonfuls of the herbs, then, after covering well the cup or bowl, allowing it to steep for several minutes by the side of the fire. The tea is sweetened to taste. Camomile tea is quite invaluable for nervousness and sleeplessness; calamus tea, for infants' colic; cinnamon tea, for hemorrhages; watermelon-seed tea, for strangury.

BONESET FOR A COUGH OR COLD (*Mrs. General Simpson*).

Pour one and one-half pints of boiling water on a ten-cent package of boneset. Let it steep at the side of the fire for ten or fifteen minutes, when strain it. Sweeten it with two and a half coffee-cupfuls of loaf-sugar, then add one half-pint of Jamaica rum; bottle it. A child should take a tea-spoonful before each meal; a grown person, a sherry-glassful.

BOTANIC COUGH SIRUP.

This book is not a medical treatise, yet I can not resist the temptation to add the following receipt, given me by Mrs. H——, of Buffalo. Many cases of long and aggravated cough have been entirely cured by its use. If the patient has a tendency to vertigo, the bloodroot may be omitted from the receipt; but for pale persons of weak vitality it will be found a valuable addition.

Ingredients: Elecampane, one ounce; spikenard, one ounce; cumfrey root, one ounce; bloodroot, one ounce; hoarhound tops, one ounce.

Add two quarts of water to these herbs, and steep them five hours in a porcelain or new tin vessel; add more boiling water, as it boils away, to keep the vessel as full as at first. At the end of this time, strain the liquid, add one pound of loaf-sugar, and boil it until it is reduced to one quart.

Dose.—A dessert-spoonful before each meal and before retiring. It should be kept in a cool place; or a little spirits may be added to prevent its spoiling.

ARRANGEMENT OF DISHES FOR INVALIDS.

BEEFSTEAK.

Cut out the tender part of the beef from a porter-house or a tenderloin steak. The slice from these steaks, if large, can be cut in two, as it is sufficient for two meals for an invalid. Let it be three-quarters of an inch thick; trim or press it into shape (it should be oval in form). Broil it carefully over a hot fire, cooking it rare: the inside should be pink, not raw. To cook it evenly without burning, turn it two or three times, but do not pierce it with a fork nor squeeze it. It does not require over two minutes to finish it. Do not put pepper and salt over it until it is cooked, as salt rubbed on fresh meat contracts the fibres and toughens it. However, as soon as it is cooked and placed on a little hot oval platter, sprinkle salt and pepper over it; then, placing a small piece of fresh butter on the top, set it into the oven a minute to allow the butter to soak into the meat: it only requires a small piece of butter. Beefsteak swimming in butter is unwholesome, and as slovenly as it is wasteful.

If an invalid can eat beefsteak, he can generally eat some one vegetable with it; and to make the little plump, tender morsel of beef look more tempting, garnish it with the vegetable. If with potatoes, bake one or two equal-sized potatoes to a turn. When quite hot, remove the inside; mash it perfectly smooth, season it with butter, or, what is better, cream and salt, and press it through a colander. It will look like vermicelli. Place it in a circle around the steak.

If with pease, when they are out of season, the French canned pease or the American brand of "Triumph" pease will be found almost as good. One can, if kept well covered, should furnish three or four meals for an invalid. Merely heat them, adding a little salt and butter. Do not use much, if any, of the juice in making a circle of them around the beef.

If you garnish with tomatoes, make them into a sauce, as follows: After cooking and seasoning them with salt and pepper, turn off the watery part, add a little stock, if you have it (however, it is nice without it, if the word stock frightens any body), and press it through the sieve. Pour it around the steak.

www.ingramcontent.com/pod-product-compliance
Lightning Source LLC
Chambersburg PA
CBHW081725100526
44591CB00016B/2499